DON'T CALL IT A MIRACLE

The Movement to Cure Spinal Cord Injury

KATE WILLETTE

DON'T CALL IT A MIRACLE:
The Movement to Cure Spinal Cord Injury
First Edition

by Kate Willette

This project was supported, in part by grant number 90PR3002, from the U.S. Administration for Community Living, Department of Health and Human Services, Washington, D.C. 20201. Grantees undertaking projects under government sponsorship are encouraged to express freely their findings and conclusions.
Points of view or opinions do not, therefore, necessarily represent official Administration for Community Living policy.

All illustrations copyright © Lisa May
Book design by Lisa May

The material contained in this book is presented for the purpose of educating and inform-ing readers about paralysis and its effects. Nothing contained herein should be construed as medical diagnosis or treatment advice. This information should not be used in place of the advice of a physician or other qualified healthcare provider. If any questions arise while reading this book, the PRC strongly recommends contacting a physician or the appropriate healthcare provider.

ISBN 978-0-9960951-2-9

For information or to request additional copies of this book:
Paralysis Resource Center
636 Morris Turnpike, Suite 3A
Short Hills, New Jersey 07078
Toll-free 1-800-539-7309
email c/o infospecialist@ChristopherReeve.org

DEDICATION

This book is dedicated to Jennifer Longdon.

Foreword

Something breaks. Tissue is scarred. Neurons die. The hours after a spinal cord injury are often described as a war zone — as the body attempts to shield itself from trauma, the delicate cord bears the brunt of the damage.

As if physical scars are not enough, we have all heard bedside horror stories of medical "professionals" who say, in those early, dark days: "Here's your chair. Here's what you can expect from life with a spinal cord injury. Get used to it. And by the way, what you get back in the first few months is all you can expect for the rest of your life."

Nonsense.

When it comes to research, spinal cord injury is often compared with disease. Retrofitting a spinal cord injury into a standard classification of a disease is not fair to the complexity of this injury or to what people living with spinal cord injury face daily. Every spinal cord injury is different, which means that there can never be a one-size-fits-all cure, but rather a series of significant breakthroughs that will eventually combine to solve this puzzle.

Christopher Reeve was injured in 1995. He used his celebrity, his considerable resources, and his astonishing intellect to put forth the idea that a cure was possible. He put 70% of what he raised into that vision; the remaining 30% went to advance the Quality of Life initiatives that Dana championed. He did not shy away from the four letter word — *hope* — and inspired the world to believe that nothing is impossible. In his early days he was often met with protest and the criticism that his campaign for a cure would diminish the hard work and real accomplishments of advocates who led the charge to pass the Americans with Disabilities Act (ADA). Like the great civil rights leaders of the 20th century, Chris met his detractors with love and compassion — but he never wavered from his message that a cure was not just possible. It was a moral imperative.

Enter Kate Willette. Inspired by the leadership of the pioneers at Unite 2 Fight Paralysis, Kate came to realize after sitting through a research presentation that there has to be a simpler and easier way to grasp the complex storylines of spinal cord research. How can a lay person with skin in the game determine what's important and what is essentially just "spin?" Even within the community we battle each other over which facts are gospel. So how was she going to sift through the many layers of scientific data and unearth the truth — the simple, unadulterated truth about the research triumphs and challenges within this field?

Why, she wondered, isn't there a sort of Research for Dummies, a "Rosetta stone" for advocates? Kate was further inspired by Michael Mangeniello, one of the earliest SCI cure warriors. Michael had co-written "Back to Basics. HIV/AIDS as a Model" with Margaret Anderson of Faster Cures. That paper is an illustrative and comprehensive account of what it took to advance awareness and resources for AIDS/HIV research. The parallels spoke to Kate.

One of the key messages? Activism and fearless determination is critical to progress, but in order to succeed, those who have the greatest stake in a cause or a mission must learn to be more sophisticated about the research.

That's the reason for this book. It's important. Like the research itself, activism will have to take many forms to move the needle and raise the resources required to the task. There must be opportunities for collaborators, room for grassroots, community, national, and international efforts — all the qualities of an effective movement. That's the way change really happens.

This book is not meant to be a period piece, but one that will be revisited regularly as progress moves forward. We need a tool to map out progress as it happens, and this book is the best idea that's come forward — we have the right person at the right time addressing a profound need. Chris said it best: *Nothing of any consequence happens unless people get behind an idea.* It begins with an individual and they share the idea with more individuals… and eventually it becomes a movement.

And movement is what it is all about.

Peter Wilderotter
President and CEO
Christopher & Dana Reeve Foundation
October, 2014

TABLE OF CONTENTS

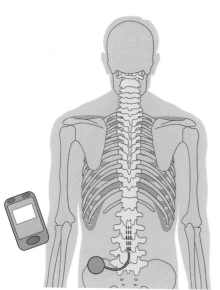

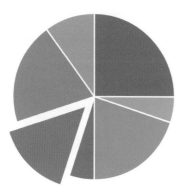

ILLUSTRATIONS

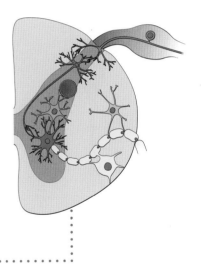

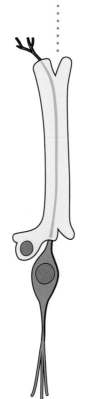

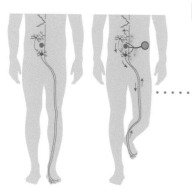

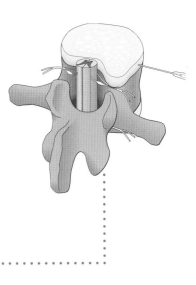

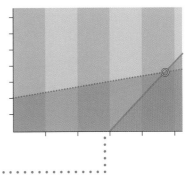

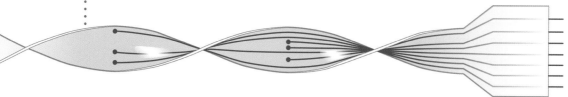

INTRODUCTION

If you're reading this, you already get why finding a cure for paralysis matters. You don't need me to tell you that it's urgent. You'd like to know what the chances for a cure really are, what the holdup is, and what — if anything — you personally can do to speed things up. Answering those three questions in a clear, objective way is what this book is for.

When you do a Google search on "cure spinal cord injury," you'll get hundreds of thousands of hits — that's hundreds of thousands of websites where there might be information about the science that could help paralyzed people get back their legs, their hands, their sex lives, and all the rest. It's amazing, especially if you keep in mind that at this moment there is no cure. Many of those Google hits will lead to websites with news stories that cover the same event over and over; some will be pitches designed to convince the uninformed to become human guinea pigs in unscientific trials; some will lead to incomprehensible papers published in academic journals that you have to pay $30 (per article!) just to read.

The good news is that there is so much information out there; the bad news is exactly the same. *There is so much information out there.* What's more, that mountain of data is always growing, so even if you could get your arms around it for a moment, you'd still be buried under an avalanche within a very short time.

Here's the thing. When you or your loved one got a spinal cord injury, you also became part of what's called a "patient group." I became a member of that patient group on March 7, 2001, at about four in the afternoon. My graceful, gifted husband had taken a weird fall at a local ski resort and broken his neck. Boom, welcome to the worst club ever. There are hundreds of thousands of us here in the USA and millions more around the world; those numbers are of course growing every minute of every day. We would all like a cure, preferably right now.

When you hear stories of medical breakthroughs, there seem to be just three kinds of plot lines. The first one focuses on the scientists — people in lab coats, toiling away until the big discovery moment arrives, often by accident. In 1928, a Scottish scientist named Alexander Fleming was working out of the basement of a London hospital. He was trying to learn more about *staph*, the bug that causes, among other things, pneumonia. Fleming was apparently something of a slob because when he went home for a long weekend one day in September, he left a collection of little dishes of *staph* out in the open air. When he got back to his lab a few days later, he could plainly see that something odd had happened. In most of the open dishes there were dots of *staph* spreading out and taking over — but in this one dish there was also a big blob of blue-green mold, and the space all around that blob was empty. *The mold was preventing the bug from growing.* That mold eventually led to the development of the drug we call penicillin. Within a few years, pneumonia had gone from number one cause of death to treatable illness. So, that's the first plot. Hardworking scientist finds or stumbles upon a cure. It does happen.

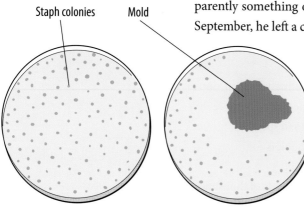

Staph colonies   Mold

The second medical breakthrough plot is about the power of love. These stories center around a single heroic member of some patient group, usually the close family member of a sick person. Remember the 1992 film, *Lorenzo's Oil*? The movie set up a storyline in which a desperate father (Augusto Odone) single-handedly educated himself, took on the established scientific community, and discovered a cure for his young son, Lorenzo. The boy had been born with a horrifying fatal condition called *adrenoleukodystrophy*, which had no cure. It was a fine dramatic film, but it wasn't true to the facts. Compelling drama needs heroes, villains, and conflict. Brilliant, desperate father. Hostile, cold doctor. *Institutional indifference and plodding scientific method kills innocent children!* That was the Hollywood version. What actually happened was that Odone — who had money to spend — began by arranging a gathering of every scientist he could find who was working on the basic biology of his son's disease. Far from dismissing him or working against him, at least one of the scientists at that conference became a close collaborator. That was Hugo Moser, a neurologist from the Kennedy Kreiger Institute in Baltimore.

The story of *Lorenzo's Oil*, as told by the screenwriters, was false and even cruel to the scientists it portrayed, but worse, it missed the point. The movie could have shown how the dad and the researcher were *both necessary*. It could have shown that the model for faster progress in medicine requires patient advocates who can learn to work with sci-entists and at the same time find ways to pressure the system in which those scientists do their jobs. That's exactly what Augusto Odone did; it would have made a hell of a story.

And that brings us to the last of the three medical breakthrough storylines, the one that is both true and helpful to us. It's a horrendous tale. When the first few American victims of AIDS began to die of aggressive cancers and pneu-monia in the summer of 1981, nobody guessed that a modern-day plague had arrived. Over the next six months there were 270 reported cases, and almost half of them had already died by Christmas.

The exact nature of the virus that led to AIDS wasn't identified until the summer of 1984, by which time almost 6,000 Americans had succumbed. When the group that called itself ACT UP was formed in the spring of 1987, the death toll stood at about 41,000, and it was accelerating quickly. ACT UP was a loose collection of self-appointed committees — ordi-nary people who were tired of watching helplessly as their loved ones (and they themselves) got sick and quickly died. It really was a plague.

Sadly, the oil that Odone helped to identify did not make his son better. In the years since doctors first began prescribing it to young patients, studies have shown that the oil cannot reverse symptoms once they've begun. Rather, it can prevent those symptoms from ever appearing, if given early enough. Dr. Moser was still working on a reliable screening test to detect the disease in young children when he died, more than 20 years after he first met Lorenzo. Lorenzo himself died at the age of 30, having lived with seizures and the inability to move or speak nearly all his days.

These people, as it turned out, changed the relationship between researchers and patients. They had nothing to lose, and they didn't have time to be scared of challenging author-ity, whether it was a faceless government agency or a sophisticated billion-dollar drug company. *They wanted to live.* Between 1987 and 1992 (while another **150,000** Americans died of AIDS and 10 million people were infected worldwide) ACT UP brought focus to their cause with a string of carefully planned, fearless public demonstrations, all designed to wake up the public.

It wasn't enough.

Within ACT UP, one of those loose committees had long been devoting itself to under-standing the science behind a possible cure. Over time, this nerdy little gang (called TAG, for Treatment Action Group) had earned the respect of both scientists and bureaucrats. They'd done their homework. They knew what they were talking about, and their members had seats at the table where decisions were made about how studies should be designed. It was a first. Those advocates had the most skin in the game, and they weren't about to see any more precious time or money wasted.

Think about the power of that model, compared to that of a lone scientist lucking into a cure, or a lone desperate family member teaching himself neurology so he could find a cure all by himself.

TAG's 1992 report asking for massive new investment in basic science and explaining how the national effort to fight AIDS should be re-structured was largely adopted by the FDA… and still it would be four more years before the first effective treatments were available. By then, 360,000 Americans had lost their lives to AIDS, as had 5.5 million others around the world. Those effective treatments grew directly out of the collaboration between TAG, the bureaucrats, and the scientists — and TAG itself grew out of a community that was determined to be part of the solution. While we can't know how long it might have taken to develop the drugs that AIDS patients take today without ACT UP and TAG, it's absolutely certain that they moved the calendar forward.

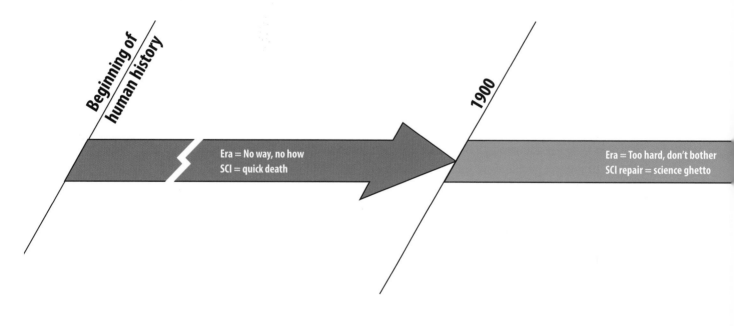

The moral of that tale? *Patient groups can matter. Successful research can be driven forward by a patient group that is **well-informed, organized, focused, creative, and relentless.***

Even a few hundred people can ramp up the speed at which research succeeds, but that won't happen unless there are people in the group who meet all those criteria. Everybody doesn't need to have every one of those qualities, but there must be enough people who have each of them. I've put *well-informed* at the top of the list, because if you don't come to the table with a solid grasp of what the basic problems are, no amount of passion, organization, bright ideas, or determination is going to get you anywhere. You'll be out there chasing rainbows, and sooner or later you'll get tired of the way they vanish no matter how hard you try. That, sadly, has been our story so far.

Helping my patient group to become well-informed, then, is the job I've signed up for here. I'm not a scientist, which is actually a good thing, for two reasons. One is that it can be hard for neurobiologists to remember what it's like not to know an axon from a lugnut. The other

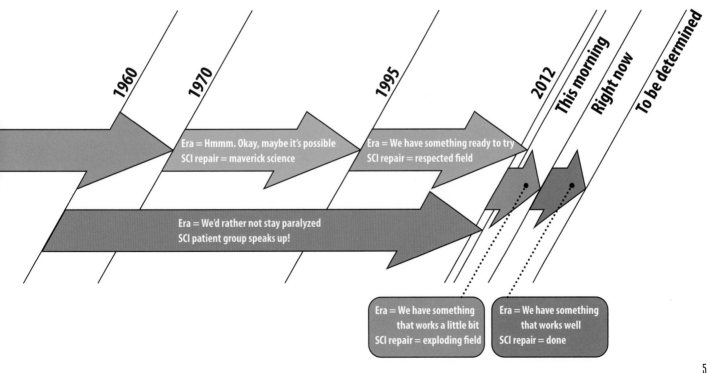

is that I want scientists to be in their labs doing science, not struggling to communicate with a lay audience.

How far is it from right now to something that works? The truth is that we don't know; it's to be determined. We don't know what the date on that last line will be. What we do know is that *we* can make it sooner rather than later.

The dream is that this book will become a platform from which we — the Spinal Cord Injury (SCI) patient group — can launch an organized, coherent and successful effort to drive research. We'll all be working from the same basic set of facts. We'll all understand enough about both science and institutional barriers to help plot a path forward.

In isolation and ignorance, all we can do is wait. But if we're informed, organized, focused, creative, and relentless, who knows? At least we have a shot.

Part One

The Stuff the Cord Is Made Of

1 The Most Basic Unit: Speakers

In the USA, the most basic unit of money is the dollar. In pitching stats, it's the earned run average. In gardening, it's the seed. In politics it's the number of votes, and in weather, it's the temperature. A basic unit is the thing that defines what you're talking about. No dollar, no money. No votes, no politician. And so on.

In your central nervous system and mine, the most basic unit is a particular kind of cell called a neuron (NUREon). Without neurons, there's no brain and no spinal cord. They're the most basic unit.

By the standards of the other human cells, neurons are pretty strange. Most cells are basically tiny little sacks of stuff. They're small factories shaped like blobs. You and I have about 200 different *kinds* of these blobs in our bodies, and most of them are easily able to reproduce themselves — the very top layer of your skin cells, for example, is completely replaced every month or so. Each of your red blood cells last about four months, and then it becomes garbage and a new one takes its place. Cells, generally, are always dividing, dying, and being born for your entire life.

But your neurons don't behave that way. Your neurons — the most basic unit of both your brain and your spinal cord — almost never divide, die off, and replace themselves.

That's fact #1. Neurons are forever. They're not supposed to die until you do.

The other news about neurons is their crazy shape. Like other cells, neurons are little bags of stuff cozied up in bunches right next to other bags of stuff just like themselves. Liver cells all hang out together and become your liver. Muscle cells, same.

To be specific, a grown up man loses about 96 million cells every minute of the day. Luckily, he also produces 96 million more to replace them. It's as if the population of New York City were 8 times as big as it is, and replaced itself 60 times an hour. The body is a busy place.

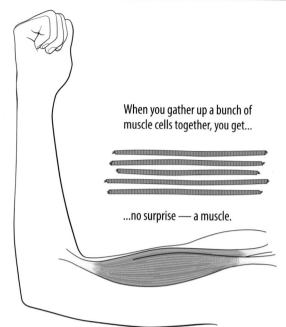

When you gather up a bunch of muscle cells together, you get...

...no surprise — a muscle.

Neurons do that too, but neurons are still lonely, in the sense that they're always prepared to talk. They even — sort of — have ears and tongues.

Okay, ears and tongues are not what scientists call them.

The ears look like little tree branches, and they're called *dendrites*. The tongues — called *axons* — are long, very slender threads with multiple branches at their tips. Dendrites can sort of "hear" what other neurons are saying. And axons are the way that neurons speak.

That's fact #2. Neurons have the job of listening and speaking. They do it with short extensions called dendrites (ears) and long ones called axons (tongues).

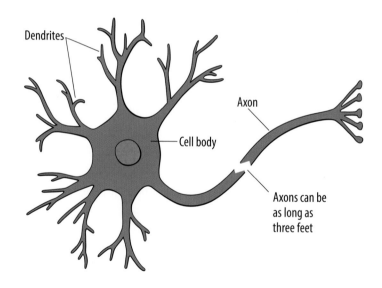

Dendrites

Axon

Cell body

Axons can be as long as three feet

Using their dendrites, they listen *only* to other neurons, always. Using their axons, though, they can speak to other neurons — but some of them can also speak *directly to muscles*. The kind of neuron that speaks to muscles is called a Motor Neuron.

Here's what the system would look like if a person had just one neuron cell body in the brain and one Motor Neuron cell body in the spinal cord. The Brain Neuron's cell body is up there in the head, safe and sound inside the skull. It has sent its axon down, down, down into the middle of the spinal cord, all the way to the bottom of the spine. That axon's job is to speak to its assigned dendrite — the listening ear of its favorite Motor Neuron. *Hello! We'd like to move the left big toe, thanks very much.*

The Motor Neuron's cell body lives deep inside the spinal cord. It has one of its many ears out waiting, just in case its favorite Brain Neuron might want it to do something. When it gets instructions, it sends the message out through its own axon, right to a waiting muscle cell on the toe. *Contract! Release! Contract!* That's right. An axon can only say two possible things to a muscle, just as a light switch can only be on or off.

It's quite amazing. By the time you could first toddle across your parents' living room, there was a vast system of connections in place. There were specific Brain Neuron voices aimed at specific Motor Neuron ears. And those Motor Neurons were attached to specific places on specific muscle cells.

That's fact #3. Almost all of the billions of connections between neurons are wired into place before birth. The circuits exist.

Your whole body works this way… individual brain cells connected to individual spinal cord cells, those cells connected to individual muscle cells, for all your life. Running, dancing, wriggling, doing downward dog or deep knee bends, whatever. All of it depends on this relay system set in place during the time you were being formed and in the first years of your life. You have about 86 billion-with-a-b neurons in your brain, and another billion in your spinal cord, which is one hell of a lot of talking and listening going on inside your body. It's why human beings can do things like play World Cup-level soccer *and* gently bathe their infant children. Our range is extreme, and it's exquisitely tuned.

If you have an injury to your spinal cord, though, those axons — the voices that have been grown and trained to descend from your brain

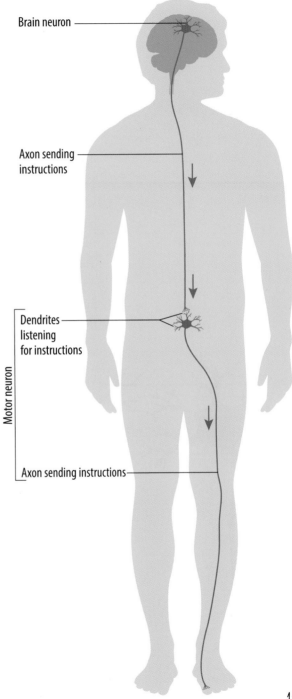

Brain neuron

Axon sending instructions

Dendrites listening for instructions

Motor neuron

Axon sending instructions

11

and lock in with their listening counterparts — are a big part of the problem. They're broken. The cell bodies — the tiny bags of stuff up in your brain — are perfectly okay. The ears they're trying to reach — the dendrites of the Motor Neurons down below — are also fine. The axons of the Motor Neurons are still right where they've always been, extending out to the muscles, and — at least at first — the muscles themselves are intact and ready to go.

Two Variations on the Basic Unit

So, that's part of the picture. We have our Brain Neurons saying *on/off* and our Motor Neurons responding by getting muscle fibers to *contract/relax*, but how does the brain know what's happening to the body? Where does sensation come from? And how are we able to react so quickly to things like stepping on a tack, before we're even aware of pain? How, for that matter, are we able to do a thing as complicated as walking without conscious thought? The answer is two more kinds of neurons.

First are Sensory Neurons. Like Motor Neurons, they have cell bodies with axons extending from them, but they don't work in quite the same way. When a Motor Neuron's dendrite gets an order from an axon, that order passes through the Motor Neuron's cell body on its way out to its own axon. But a Sensory Neuron's cell body is by-passed by the whole operation. The Sensory Neuron is shaped sort of like a dead end T-intersection, with the cell body in the dead end, and a pair of axons going off in two directions away from it. There's no dendrite — no apparatus for taking in information from other neurons — at all.

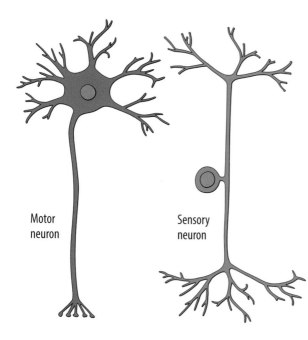

Motor
neuron

Sensory
neuron

One of the Sensory Neuron axons heads out into your body, where it's attached to a particular part of you — say, the bottom of your toe. At the end of that axon are *receptors*, each one sort of like a microscopic antenna. Every receptor is tuned to its own frequency; it can "hear" the difference between an itch, a sharp poke, a tickle, or a caress. When the signal is the sort that it's been tuned to hear, the receptor shoots that information directly back to your spinal cord, where one of a number of things can happen.

First is that the information rides the axon up into the cord, passes by the Sensory Neuron cell body, and zips along the other side of the T all the way up into the brain. What happens there is — you guessed it — the dendrite of Brain Neuron is already wired in place to hear the news from this particular end of this particular Sensory Neuron. This is how it works when the sensation is the sort that tells you the shape and texture of whatever is touching your toe.

Another possibility is that you have stepped on a tack. When that happens, a different receptor from a neighboring Sensory Neuron will grab the news, and again it will shoot up the axon and into the cord. This time, though, that Sensory Neuron's axon will have a built-in split. One part will head up into the brain, but the other one will make the fastest possible connection (up to 250 mph) with the Motor Neurons needed to get your muscles activated so your foot lifts up. The problem is that Sensory Neurons can't talk directly to Motor Neurons. Enter the *Interneuron*, the fourth and last kind.

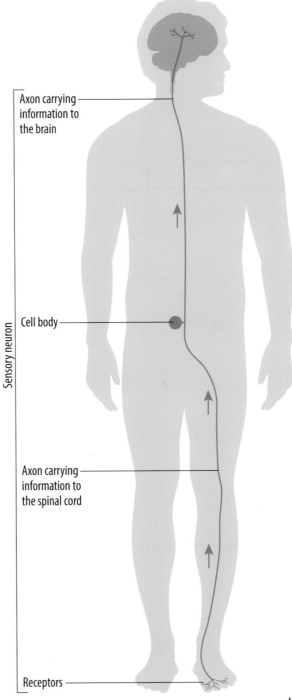

Axon carrying information to the brain

Sensory neuron

Cell body

Axon carrying information to the spinal cord

Receptors

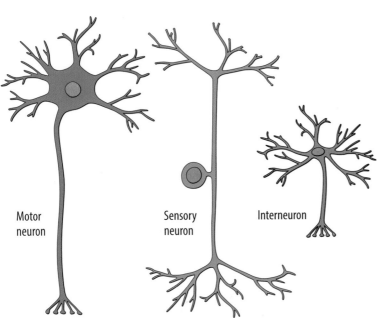

Motor neuron

Sensory neuron

Interneuron

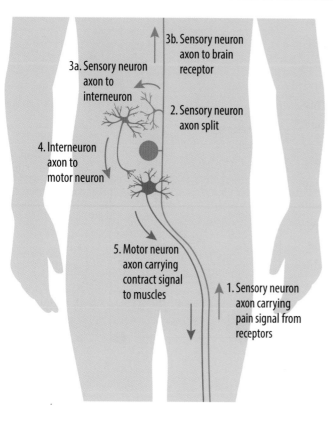

3b. Sensory neuron axon to brain receptor

3a. Sensory neuron axon to interneuron

2. Sensory neuron axon split

4. Interneuron axon to motor neuron

5. Motor neuron axon carrying contract signal to muscles

1. Sensory neuron axon carrying pain signal from receptors

Interneurons are like very, very fast translators — they're go-betweens. They take the information from Sensory Neurons (*TACK!!*) and zap it right to dendrites of nearby Motor Neurons — the ones that control the muscles you need to jerk your foot back. The brain isn't involved until a tiny fraction of a second later, which is the time it takes for the other split of that Sensory Neuron's axon to shoot all the way up the cord and get connected with receptors inside the brain. (*That hurts!!*) Your cord is jam-packed with Interneurons, from top to bottom.

And yet another possibility is that you are in the middle of the rhythmic cycle we call "walking." In that case a massive boatload of connections between millions of Sensory Neurons, Motor Neurons, and Interneurons will function as a single super-efficient unit. Responding to feedback not from your brain but rather from deep inside the lower part of your spinal cord, all those cells create a reliable pattern of firing between axons and dendrites. The phrase we use to refer generally to collections of connected cells is *Pattern Generator*. The pattern generator in your lower spinal cord is what keeps your feet, ankles, knees, and hips in easy, synchronized motion.

So what does a spinal cord actually look like? It's about a foot and a half long. At the top and the bottom, it's as thick as the tip of your pinky finger, and maybe half that wide in the middle. If you wound it up in a coil and held it in one hand, it would weigh about the same as five US nickels.

If you cut through a hunk of it like a piece of sushi or a jellyroll, what would you see? It would be shaped like a slightly flattened circle. You'd see a sort of muddled fat gray H in the center, and that H would be surrounded by thick white stuff.

The fat gray part is full of Motor Neuron and Interneuron cell bodies. The Sensory Neuron cell bodies are all outside the cord itself, tucked into little swellings called *ganglia*. The white stuff all around the H is actually made of long bundles of hundreds of millions of axons, each and every one of them snug inside a white coating called *myelin*. That's your cord.

A slender tube that weighs almost nothing and does almost everything.

Why do we care what these cells look like and how they work? Because we want to understand what has been damaged and what is intact. Remember those AIDS activists? This is what Dr. Anthony Fauci, one of the scientists at the National Institutes of Health said about them:

> *They elevated themselves by their own self-education on these things. And then it became very clear that you weren't going to mess with these people, because they knew exactly what you were talking about — and they knew exactly what they were talking about.*
>
> from the film, *How to Survive a Plague*, 2012, directed by David France

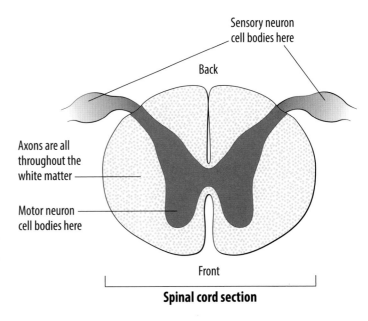

Sensory neuron cell bodies here

Back

Axons are all throughout the white matter

Motor neuron cell bodies here

Front

Spinal cord section

We don't need PhDs in neurobiology. We just need to know what we're talking about.

There are, as it happens, a couple of other cell types inside the spinal cord, each of which is important enough to get its own chapter, so that's what's coming next. For now, though, just notice that **knowing what's going on with the neurons** has led to some of the most promising research strategies.

1. **Knowledge**: Unlike most other cells, neurons don't automatically replace themselves when they're damaged or killed.
   Strategy: *We might need replacements for the Interneuron and Motor Neuron cell bodies that were lost at the injury site.* There are scientists working on this one all over the world. We'll look at what they're doing in the chapter about Replacement.

2. **Knowledge**: Neurons' connections to one another and to the rest of the body are all hooked up and don't change easily.
   Strategy: *We might need to do some creative "re-wiring."* This is another hot area for research all over the planet. We'll cover it in the chapter about Reconnection.

3. **Knowledge**: Neurons' axons don't know how to grow past the injury site and back to where they were before the injury.

   Strategy: *We might need to figure out how to help them do so.* And this one falls into the world of Regeneration.

That right there is how good research science starts. First you do enough basic work to understand what you're up against, and then you figure out a mechanism to fix what's wrong. The more basic knowledge you have, the better your plans will be.

2 The Indispensable Wrapper Cells

Back in January of 2009, a California company called Geron (JAIR-un) announced that it was going to be putting living cells into the bodies of a few people with new spinal cord injuries. After years of asking, they'd finally gotten permission from the US government to see if what had worked on the rats they'd tested in their labs would also work on human beings.

It was a big day. Millions of people had seen those rats on television five years earlier, scrabbling contentedly around in their cages. *Paralyzed, then not paralyzed.* How could this be possible? Had scientists figured out how to replace lost rat neurons? Or how to make their broken axons grow and form the right connections?

No.

Neurons are the basic unit in the spinal cord, but they're not the only kind of cell that lives there, and they're definitely not the only one that matters. The one we're going to focus on now is the one the Geron trial was aimed at replacing. Its scientific name is a six-syllable mouthful: *oligodendrocyte* (oh-liggo-DEN-droh-site). I call it a wrapper cell.

Axons aren't naked, or at least the ones that work right aren't. Instead, they have a sort of staggered wrapping. If you could make yourself extremely tiny, like 15,000 times smaller than you are, you'd be small enough to get a close look along the length of a working axon. What you'd see is that it looks like a lane divider in a swimming pool — a long, strong rope strung closely with white, American-football-shaped floats. There are tiny spaces between each pair of floats, and as it turns out, those tiny spaces are the actual locations where signals travel.

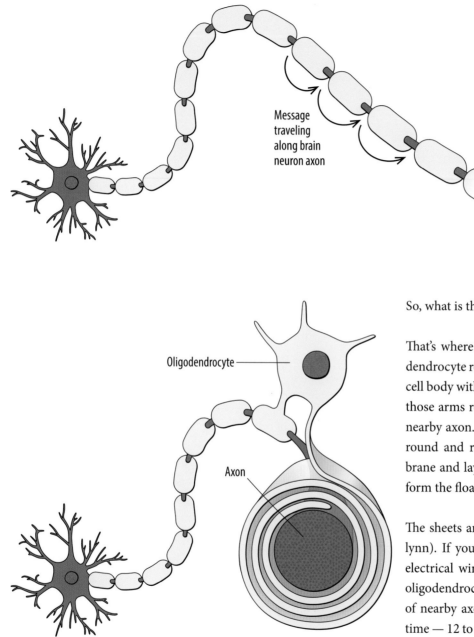

Message traveling along brain neuron axon

Oligodendrocyte

Axon

Yes, this means that only a very small fraction of your run-of-the-mill axon is *ever used to move messages*; in a sense, the axon is only there to support the floats that create those tiny spaces, which are called *Nodes of Ranvier*. When a message travels down from a brain neuron toward a motor neuron, it's actually hopping along from node to node, skipping right over the floats. Without the floats, the signal crawls, or stalls altogether. No message, no movement.

So, what is that float? And how does it get there?

That's where the wrapper cells come in. The oligodendrocyte reminds me of an octopus. It's a wild little cell body with as many as 50 "arms," and every one of those arms reaches out to find an empty space on a nearby axon. Then the wrapping begins. Round and round and round, the arm extends its own membrane and lays down winding sheets of coating that form the float.

The sheets are made of stuff called *myelin* (MY-uh-lynn). If you like the idea of the axon as a sort of electrical wire, this stuff is the insulation. A single oligodendrocyte can build little wrappers on dozens of nearby axons, and it does that over a very short time — 12 to 18 hours. Once it's finished, it's finished; it's not going to be finding another axon to wrap a few days later, or ever.

Are these cells like neurons, in the sense that they don't reproduce themselves? Are we born with all the oligodendrocytes we're ever going to have? Yes and no.

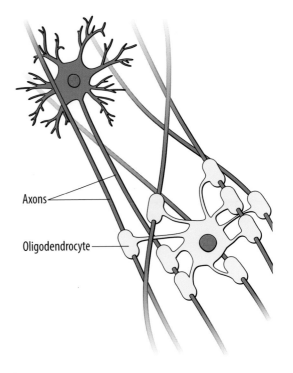

During the early weeks of gestation — often before our mothers even knew they were pregnant — one of the things that was happening is that the cells that would become *us* were getting branched into different paths. At the very beginning, there was just one cell: the fertilized egg. Very quickly — right away, in fact — it started to divide and divide and divide, sorting itself as it did into groups.

To picture this, think about a tree branching. The trunk is the first blob of cells, all alike. They form a ball. Pretty soon the cells that make up the ball start to become different from one another, in layers. The cells in the outermost layer of that ball are all destined to become one of these things: skin, eyes, other sensory organs, or part of the nervous system, but they're a long way from making their final commitments. At the beginning they're all the same, with all the same options. They exist on one major branch leaving the original trunk, the outermost layer of cells on the ball.

Pretty soon some of them commit to becoming part of the nervous system. They could become neurons, or oligodendrocytes, (or the third kind of nervous system cell that we still have to talk about), but they can't become anything else. The door to becoming cells that become eyes *and* cells that become skin officially closes. They're committed. At this stage in their lives, those cells are called *neural stem cells*. They're "stem" because they're not totally branched yet and they can still reproduce themselves. They're "neural" because they're definitely going to be some part of the nervous system.

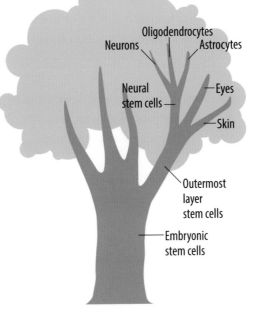

Okay. So you can guess what happens next: some of the neural stem cells split off to become neurons, and some split off to become oligodendrocytes. But the interesting thing is that some of them sort of get half way to oligodendrocyte and stop there. These are called *oligodendrocyte precursors* (OPCs). They're like vice-presidents. They can't go back and become something else, and they won't go forward and become oligodendrocytes *unless they're needed*. It's just like the way the vice-president stays a vice-president unless the president dies, in which case he or she moves up. The OPCs are in the brain and in the spinal cord in case of emergency.

What would be an emergency? Well, if for some reason a regular oligodendrocyte died, there would be a replacement. Unfortunately, there aren't enough OPCs in the spinal cord to replace all the ones that are lost in a major catastrophe, like a spinal cord injury. But they do exist, and even in an adult body they do know how to finish their growing, become oligodendrocytes, and wrap axons with myelin. By way of contrast, we don't have any version of this for neurons. There are no "neuron precursors" standing by to take the place of lost neurons in the spinal cord.

People who have multiple sclerosis are also suffering from lost myelin. In their case, their own immune systems attack and destroy the myelin that coats axons in their brain neurons. No one knows why. For them, replacing the myelin isn't enough because their own bodies see it as poison.

What Geron did in that 2009 trial was this: They started in their lab with cells from the "trunk," which are known as *embryonic stem cells*. The cells they had could still become anything in the body. In the lab, Geron scientists meticulously re-created the process by which cells move to the *neural stem cell* branch. Then they pushed those cells toward the oligodendrocyte branch, just to the place where they weren't quite "cooked." They were OPCs. Vice-presidents.

Then they spent many years doing animal studies to prove that putting these cells into paralyzed people would be safe. Then they spent years and years convincing the US FDA that those animal studies meant the cells might work in humans. Then the FDA said, "Okay." And then Geron recruited the first few patients. And finally, they put a small dose of their cells into real people with complete spinal cord injuries. The cells Geron put into those patients were OPCs.

The idea was to get the OPC cells to turn into oligodendrocytes and hope that they would build new bundles of myelin along whatever axons had survived the injury. Scientists have known for a long time now that there are usually lots of axons still in place after an injury, but they don't work right because they've lost their little white bundles of myelin. We're going to talk a lot more about that trial and what happened to it later; for now we just want to understand the thinking behind it.

The Geron scientists knew that our adult bodies are used to having OPCs in them, because we all have them. Whatever chemistry is going on inside our brains and our spinal cords, it's a friendly place for OPCs. OPCs know how to finish off their growing under the right circumstances; they know how to step up and take over for dead oligodendrocytes, which is just exactly what paralyzed people need to happen. The new wrapper cells might just be able to wrap enough axon segments to build up a whole new set of nodes. Bingo, connection restored. The concept made sense, and it definitely worked in those rats. Will it work in people? Stay tuned.

Here's an interesting thing: the axons that run out from your cord and into your arms and legs *also* are like strings studded with myelin floats, but these floats aren't put there by oligodendrocytes. Those arm and leg axons are part of the *peripheral nervous system*, which is called that because it's on the *periphery* — it's outside the center, where your cord is.

In the peripheral system, the cells that make myelin are called *Schwann cells*. They don't do their thing with little arms extending out from their cell bodies; instead, the Schwann cell just wraps its whole self all around a chunk of axon. Each Schwann cell can make as many as 100 wraps, around and around and around. And every layer is coated with myelin, like butter and cinnamon inside the layers of a cinnamon roll before you twist it up. It might take as many as 3,000 Schwann cells to make enough myelin floats for a single foot-long axon

The one thing that most people know about the difference between the central nervous system (CNS) and the peripheral nervous system (PNS) is that damage to the first is permanent, but damage to the second is not. How does the PNS pull this off?

Schwann cells. It turns out that these cells have a whole bag of tricks. They wrap themselves into little balls of myelin, sure, but they also have other hats to wear. Think of the bundles of axons that make the calf muscle in your leg move. They come from motor neurons that have their cell bodies in your spinal cord, and they're attached at the other end to the muscles of your lower leg.

Suppose you crash your bicycle on wet pavement someplace and slide into the metal edge of a fence. A deep gash in your leg slices through the nerves that attach to your calf muscles. Ouch, goodbye to sensation and movement in that muscle for a while.

Bundles of axons go by two different names, depending on where they are. If the bundle is in the white matter inside your spinal cord, it's called a **tract**. If it's a bundle that leaves the cord and runs out into one of your limbs, it's called a **nerve**. **Nerve** is the name we give to a collection of axons that all go to the same muscle.

Luckily, your Schwann cells have a plan to fix all that. When the axons they've wrapped themselves around get damaged, Schwann cells don't just give up and wither away, like oligodendrocytes do in the spinal cord. Instead, they do this amazing transformer thing, where instead of clinging desperately to the dying axon, they re-shape themselves to form a sort of tunnel. The tunnel is a surface for the broken stub of the axon to travel along, aiming straight at the old target muscle. Inside the tunnel they've built, the Schwann cells are also pumping out *growth factors* — molecules that are like vitamins to the axon. It takes time, and if the distance from the gash to the target muscle is long there will be mistakes in direction, but usually this system results in getting back both lost sensation and movement. Once the axon is safely growing toward its muscle, the Schwann cell turns back into a wrapper so that signals can travel. Handy little thing!

The obvious question is, can Schwann cells work in the spinal cord, too? Can they help damaged axons in there grow their way back to their old targets, and can they do the wrapping work that lost oligodendrocytes can't? If they could, we'd be looking at a possible therapy. One thing that might make this option even better than the OPC plan is that this is a cell-based fix that would use your own cells. OPCs have to come from another source, which means your body might reject them. But Schwann cells are in your arms and legs right now. Your body would recognize them as *you* and not something foreign that had to be destroyed.

Either way, we're going to need some myelin. We're going to need it for the axons that have managed to survive the injury but can't conduct signals, and we're going to need it when scientists figure out a way to get the broken axons to grow back.

Down in Florida, there's a group of spinal cord injury researchers at a place called The Miami Project to Cure Paralysis; they've spent most of the last 30 years working out all the issues around how to use Schwann cells. They finally began the first trials of their cells in paralyzed people in 2013. In the chapter about how clinical trials work, we'll look at the details of that one.

3   MANAGEMENT AND MAINTENANCE TEAM

The next time you pass through an airport, pay attention to how many people and structures it takes to make the place run safely and efficiently. Outside, there are parking garages, traffic control cops, curbs, etc. where passengers get picked up and dropped off, stands of carts, and baggage handlers. Inside, there are restaurants, bookshops, bathrooms, and bars. There are conveyor belts, escalators, trains, and electric carts for hauling all those people around.

Flight attendants take tickets, cashiers sell snacks, ground crews refuel aircraft, and maintenance people keep the building clean. Somewhere nearby there are air traffic controllers making sure that the planes land and take off in an orderly way. It's like a giant organism with a thousand moving pieces, each one doing its part to keep the whole shebang healthy and functional.

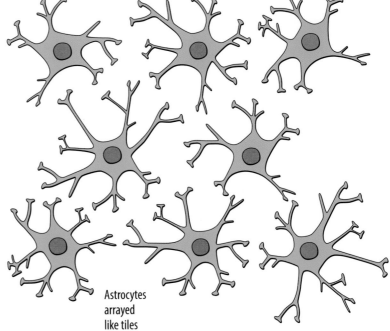

Astrocytes arrayed like tiles

The last kind of central nervous system cells we're going to talk about are — to your body — sort of like that collection of airport employees is to the airport. The cells are called *astrocytes* because they're shaped like stars. When your spinal cord is functioning the way it's meant to, there are billions of them living and working in your spinal cord, neatly arrayed like so many tiny tiles. Each one has between five and ten "arms" that normally don't overlap or touch one another. Astrocytes can split and reproduce, but they're not the kind of cells that wear out and have to replace themselves every few weeks, like skin cells.

What are they good for? Like the people employed by airport restaurants, they feed the central nervous system. *Protoplasmic* astrocytes hang out in your cord's gray matter between neuron cell bodies and the outsides of the vessels that carry nutritious neuron food in your blood. They can tell when your neurons are extra busy, and they can make your blood vessels a little thicker and get more blood flowing at those times, just as a Starbucks manager can make sure there's plenty of French Roast on hand during the morning commuter rush. During slow times, astrocytes can save energy in your body by shrinking those same blood vessels.

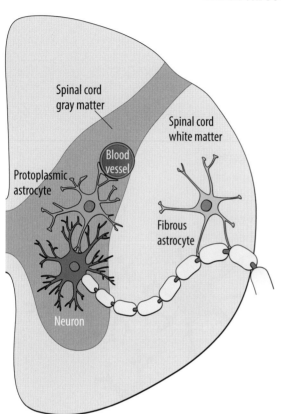

Spinal cord gray matter

Spinal cord white matter

Blood vessel

Protoplasmic astrocyte

Fibrous astrocyte

Neuron

Fibrous astrocytes are all over the white matter, sending their arms out to touch the nodes between blobs of myelin on your axons.

They're smart little buggers. Every time one of your dendrites connects with an axon's receptor, there's an arm of an astrocyte right there, checking to make sure the connection is strong and supplying a boost of whatever's needed to keep it that way. They also tailor their behavior depending on where exactly they are in your spinal cord, sort of in the same way that flight attendants working the first class section of a flight to France would behave differently than they would working the cabin of a flight to Disneyland.

I'm leaning heavily on this airport analogy for two reasons: One is that it's simple to understand, and it would be an unnecessary distraction to explain exactly *how* astrocytes manage to do all their various jobs; it's enough to know that they're key players, needed for both structure and function. The other is that the airport idea helps make it obvious what happens when something goes terribly wrong.

On the morning of September 11, 2001, the very first thing the people in charge of New York's air traffic control did was to stop any more planes from taking off. That was the easy part. The hard part came next: safely landing every last one of the 3,949 planes that were in the air already. In the comparison I'm making, the planes in the air are the messages traveling along your connected neurons just before injury.

The very first thing that happens after a spinal cord injury is that all the communication stops cold, even if the injury isn't complete. *No more planes take off.* Sometimes this is called spinal shock — a short period during which everything below the injury site goes quiet.

During that period, astrocytes — like those frantic airport employees — work like mad. They call in reinforcements. They stop traffic up and down the cord because they don't know what's going on, only that something unforeseen and potentially fatal has happened. They're responding to an emergency, and one for which they're extremely well-equipped.

After an injury, astrocytes produce molecules that essentially build a wall around the damaged bit of the cord, and that's the only thing that prevents the entire cord from becoming one giant injury site. It's not the same as when, for example, you break your leg. The break in your leg is not going to spread from the point of fracture up into the bone above or below. It's going to hurt, and it's going to need to be repaired, but the damage is whatever it is, confined to the original break.

Here's how my husband described his sensation just after he fell: "I knew when I landed exactly what had happened to me. My body was numb — in fact it felt like I was lying on the snow with my feet in an impossible position, in the air. It was the position they must have been in when the fracture happened, like a switch was flipped off."

The cord doesn't work that way because it's supposed to exist inside a tightly sealed environment. The seal is called the *Blood Spinal Cord Barrier*; along with its counterpart, the *Blood Brain Barrier*, it protects your central nervous system from your own blood.

What? Yes. The cells in your spinal cord and brain — the neurons and oligodendrocytes — have never met any of the cells in the rest of your body. They're not ever supposed to come in contact with any of those cells, and certainly not with the cells that form your blood.

Scientists figured this out about 100 years ago, by accident. One of them injected bright blue dye into the body of an animal. Later he saw that everything inside that animal *except* its brain and spinal cord had absorbed the dye and turned blue. He figured that he hadn't used enough dye and missed the significance of this. A couple of years later one of his students injected the same dye directly into the cord. This time *only* the brain and the cord turned blue. *Oh! The body and the central nervous system aren't in touch with one another.*

So, what happens when something breaks that seal? To your body, it feels like a foreign substance has arrived. Invaders are on the premises. And so your immune system kicks in and tries to destroy the invaders, which it doesn't realize are actually *you*.

And that means you lose more cells. You lose more sensation and movement, maybe, from your own immune system's reaction than from the original injury itself.

While your immune system is busy chewing up axons and myelin as fast as possible, your astrocytes are churning out special protein-sugar chain molecules that will wall off the damage. One of the scientist names for those protein-sugar chain molecules is *proteoglycans*.

On September 11th, airport managers couldn't know exactly what was going on. How many planes did the hijackers have? Which airports were they planning to work from? At O'Hare in Chicago, authorities trying to keep people safe made a plan that reminds me of the astrocyte response to trauma: they fired up all 187 of their giant snowplows and used them to form a perimeter around the base of the control tower, blades pointed outward.

That's something like what astrocytes are doing when they build that wall of proteoglycans, and for a very similar reason: they can't tell what's just happened. They only know that there's danger and that they need to set up a perimeter. The difference is that astrocytes are walling the threat *inside*, which is how they protect the rest of the spinal cord. The O'Hare managers were trying to wall the threat *outside* in order to protect their traffic control towers.

Here's the problem, though. When it was clear that there was no danger to anybody in O'Hare, the snowplows were put back in storage until the winter snows arrived. But once the astrocytes have built their little wall, it's very hard to break down again. Sometimes this wall is called the *glial scar*. It's both a physical scar, like the one you probably have from the time you skinned your knee when you were five, and a chemical one.

And growing axons get stuck in it.

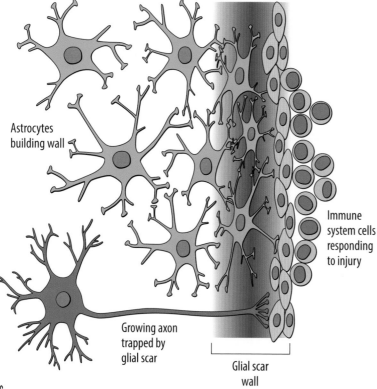

Astrocytes building wall

Immune system cells responding to injury

Growing axon trapped by glial scar

Glial scar wall

The axons that got trashed when my husband broke his neck could actually grow back, if not for that scar that his astrocytes built all around the site of his injury at the sixth vertebrae in his neck. Instead they run into those proteoglycans and turn away. I've seen videos taken in labs, where the growing tip of an axon moves through a dish of some growth medium that has a pile of CSPGs (chondroitin sulfate proteoglycans) in the middle. The axon grows its way up to the rim of that pile, does a little U-turn, and stops cold. It's not dead, but it's not going anywhere near that scar.

So where are we? We have the cord, which is made of three basic cell types: neurons, oligodendrocytes, and astrocytes. There are three kinds of neurons: motor neurons, sensory neurons, and interneurons. I've made it sound as if these things exist and function as individual units — connected to one another, yes, but in an each-man-for-himself sort of way.

Sometimes reading science is like trying to make sense of a Russian novel, where every character has four different names. The protein-sugar chain molecules go by three names. Their full name is **chondroitin sulfate proteoglycan.** Sometimes that gets turned into its acronym, CSPG. And sometimes they're called **proteoglycans** for short. When your **nickname** is five syllables long, people have a right to be annoyed. Just sayin'.

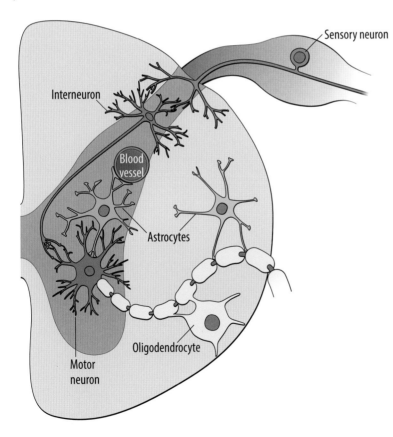

Sensory neuron

Interneuron

Blood vessel

Astrocytes

Oligodendrocyte

Motor neuron

That's not exactly how it works though. It turns out that they also gang up together in what's called a *neural network*. Taking advantage of the networks is where some of the most interesting and promising new research is going on right now.

4 Teaching a Computer to Play Checkers

Would it be possible to program a computer to learn like an ordinary eight-year-old human? Summertime, the back porch. A game of checkers. There's the red and black board, my older brother's side and my side. He moves. I jump. It's a mistake, because I've set myself up to lose four men. Click, click, click, click, off they go. I won't do that again. This process is one of the things we mean by the word *learning* — paying attention to what gives the desired result and what doesn't, and then holding onto that information so you can use it when the time comes.

Learning, in this sense, is strictly a brain thing. It's about being able to see patterns and remember them later. There's also learning going on in the body, though. When Serena and Venus Williams practiced swinging their tennis rackets, they weren't just building strength. They were training their muscles to perform certain tasks in very precise ways. They served and returned thousands of balls, until all the small motions combined to become one smooth, integrated act, done without conscious thought.

How does that work? *Neural networks*. When we're learning any new physical skill, whether it's standing up or walking or driving the Indy 500, our neurons are working amongst themselves to build structures that can function as coordinated units. Billions of neurons fire in a circuit. This one goes on, which tells that one to go off, which tells another one to go on; all in a flash, but all in a very tightly integrated way.

When the IT guys cracked the problem of getting a computer to play checkers, they did it by imitating what us humans do when we learn. They built an *artificial* neural network (ANN) that mimics one of the human kinds. The ANN adjusts itself as it goes — tweaks its own circuits in response to events outside. It learns slowly compared to my third-grade self, but it does learn. It started out just as I did, randomly following memorized rules to move my checkers around. And just like me, it lost every game.

At first.

But every time it played, it had a little more history — a little more *memory* — of what the opponent was likely to do, until after thousands and thousands of games it began to win. The ANN design had allowed it to respond — to *rewire its own circuitry* so that its playing became strategic and not random. Our brains do exactly this, and, it turns out, so do our spinal cords. The cord is not just a tube full of signals coming from the brain. It's an *extension* of the brain, made of the same kinds of cells and able to build up networks using the same kinds of rules.

I said earlier that the 86 billion neurons in our brains and spinal cords have formed connections that are meant to last all of our lives, but I didn't say how they got that way, or whether they *can* ever be changed once they're in place. It's one thing to know that they're not *supposed* to have to change — but quite another to ask if it's possible at all.

The process of forming our networks of connections starts before we're born and goes on at an insane pace for the first five years of our lives. In the years between your birth and the day you started kindergarten, your neurons were setting up links with other neurons at the rate of between 700 and 1,000 links *per second*.

Inside your spinal cord and mine, then, there are vast, complicated networks. We learned as children how to stand up, and how to stay standing, but that doesn't mean that we consciously considered the muscle groups that we needed to get to our feet and then activated them. It means that during the process of our early attempts, our neurons formed the necessary networks to make standing possible, all by themselves. They responded to feedback that they were already primed to recognize.

In a way, the baby version of you was constantly doing exactly what the checkers-playing computer was doing as it played: randomly making moves and forming circuits that led to the desired results. If you've ever seen a toddler learning to get a bite of ice cream into her own mouth, you know what this looks like. What's actually going on

It helps me to think of the growing central nervous system in terms of the internet. Each individual neuron is a webpage. Each hyperlink to that webpage — each specific connection between it and some other webpage — is a synapse. So, we start out with 86 billion webpages, and what we do before age five is create networks of connections between them.

in her young body is that her neurons are forming themselves into networks — collections of connections that all function together like the many sections in a giant orchestra. Strings, brass, woodwinds, basses, percussion, piano, harp. They make music by playing the notes of their own parts in careful synchronization with one another. Your neural networks are a little like that.

Remember the loop we talked about between a sensory neuron, an interneuron, and a motor neuron? In a healthy spinal cord, there are billions of connections like that. Information circles through them all day long, and the networks handle it smoothly without any interference or input from the brain.

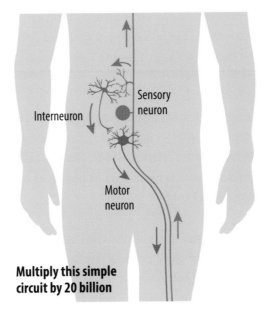

Interneuron

Sensory neuron

Motor neuron

Multiply this simple circuit by 20 billion

It makes sense if you think about it. Walking — even just standing — is a spectacularly complex activity. In each of your hips there are four different muscle "groups" — front, back, inner, and outer. The front group alone (the collection of muscles that lets you lift your knees) has six different muscles. Each of them has to move in a way that's coordinated with the others *and* with the dozens of other muscles from the back and side groups. Each of them has to be activated by millions of axons, all firing in sync.

And that's just your hip. It has to work collaboratively with all the muscle groups in your knees, ankles, feet, and toes. Things need to happen in a very particular sequence, from your heel hitting the floor, to loading that foot, to pushing off with its toes, to swinging through the stride. From the perspective of your spinal cord, walking is an elaborately choreographed activity, like millions of football game half-time dancers performing a precise routine with perfect timing. And yet most babies master it long before they can speak in sentences.

Wait. Why, then, can't we still walk after a spinal cord injury? Why don't those intact circuits work in cases where there's damage to just one tiny little part of the upper cord? Is the brain involved or not?

That's what neural network research is about: the possibility of taking advantage of whatever circuits are intact in order to steal back as much of our lost function as we can. If there are ways to use the fact that neurons can form new connections in response to feedback, it makes sense to figure out how. If there are circuits in place that need some kind of trigger to get back into action, it would help to know what those triggers are and how to activate them.

The name scientists give to one of those neural networks — the one in the lumbar part of the spinal cord — is *Central Pattern Generator (CPG)*. I don't like this name. It sounds too much as if it refers to a solid physical thing — maybe the distributor in my dad's old Pontiac. It sounds like a discrete bundle of cells that hangs out in some easy-to-find spot in the spinal cord.

In fact, what they call the CPG is really millions of coupled neurons that are linked all over the place inside a few segments of the cord, and most of those neurons are also doing other jobs at the same time they're contributing to that particular neural network. I'm saying, it's not a *thing* you could point at so much as a *function* you can describe. Also, calling it The CPG makes it sound like it's unique, when in fact there are many, many neural networks operating in our bodies.

If I were in charge, I'd re-name it the spinal locomotor pattern generator. Anyway.

The CPG is with us at birth, like the ability to breathe — and both of these networks are organized around rhythm. Your natural walk is rhythmic, just like your natural breath. The neural networks that form rhythmic activity are called pattern generators because that's their function — to create repeatable patterns of movement and behavior that require no conscious thought.

How do neural networks interact with one another? They're a little like a series of blindfolded orchestra sections; they "sense" activity in nearby sections and respond to it by playing their own instruments. I'm putting quotes around the word "sense" because I don't want to make

You can see the CPG at work in a newborn child. Hold the baby under his arms and dangle him over a flat surface so that one of his feet just touches. You'll see his legs begin to take alternate steps, just as if he somehow already knows a little about walking. In a way, he does.

it sound like spinal cord neural networks have consciousness in the same way brains do.

We sense things. We *feel* them, like hunger for example. We know the name of this feeling, and if we're lucky we can go get a cheeseburger to take care of it. The neural networks I'm talking about in the spinal cord are acting sort of like this when they respond to what other nearby neural networks are doing. They "know," for example, exactly what's happening in your lower limbs. Weight-bearing on the left foot, swinging the right leg from the hip? The neural network is organizing your right foot to get ready to do its heel strike. It can "sense" what the system is doing and anticipate what ought to happen next. In that way, it's like my young self anticipating my brother's traps on the game board. But our spinal neural networks aren't part of consciousness, because for that you need the brain.

Why do we need to talk about neural networks now? Because this part of the book is designed to capture the most basic parts of the puzzle of repairing a damaged spinal cord. We're trying to name the problem as clearly and carefully as we possibly can. This means not just "signals can't get through," but *why* exactly not. What in particular are the structures and routines that have been interrupted or impaired?

So far we have three kinds neurons: motor neurons, sensory neurons, and interneurons. We have the two kinds of wrapper cells that insulate the axons and allow them to be super-fast

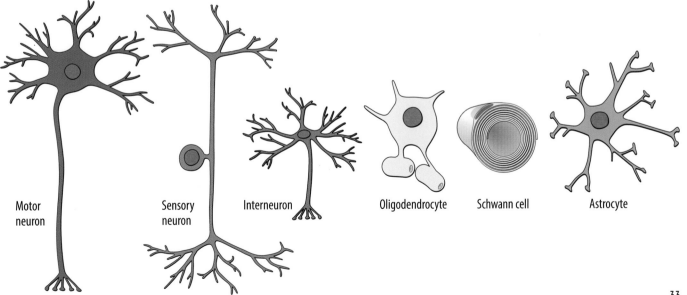

| Motor neuron | Sensory neuron | Interneuron | Oligodendrocyte | Schwann cell | Astrocyte |

at conducting messages. And we have the astrocytes, doing management and maintenance inside the cord.

Each of these cells and the work that they do — or fail to do, after injury — is going to be part of any eventual cure or therapy. They're all crucial in their own way.

But there are also the neural networks that *collections* of these cells have formed. And one of the most surprising and promising things that's ever happened in spinal cord science is happening as I write this, in the summer of 2014. It has to do with the way our neural networks can apparently respond to certain kinds of stimulus.

They can learn. Neural networks in the spinal cord can learn, just as you and I can learn to play a board game. They can change their own circuitry and structure in response to input from outside the body. They can form new functional connections. What we have in the lower spinal cord is, amazingly, a system that has the ability to rewire itself and thus restore certain functions, even without ever making contact with the brain. All we have to do is figure out how to give the networks the right input.

And that brings us to the approach called Rehabilitation, by which I emphatically do *not* mean that thing where they teach you how to live in a wheelchair.

5 PAUSE FOR CLARITY

When I was thinking about how to structure this book, I happened to run across a website where people in chairs were talking amongst themselves about "the cure." One young man was writing from Panama, telling the group about what he was calling his stem cell treatment. He was staying at a hotel in Panama City, which is at the southern end of the Panama Canal.

His family had funded this adventure to the tune of $30,000 for the first round of implants, with multiple return visits expected at $21,000 each. The young man was not yet five months post-injury when he made his first trip. He knew the names of the cells he'd been given, but to me he seemed fuzzy about why they might be working. His understanding was that they'd been tried in rats with impressive results. He swore that he'd met many people with spinal cord injuries who were getting better.

And he definitely thought the cells were working in his own body, even though he was aware that the changes he was seeing might be due to natural return. To him, the financial gamble was proving to be worth the aggravation of travel and the pain of surgery. Given that his parents were able to come up with the money, that calculation makes a kind of sense.

Why not try, if you can afford it?

That was the moment where the shape of this book began to form. Here was a family prepared to spend $100,000 on a treatment that came with absolutely no guarantee that it would work — no promise, even, that it would do no harm. Here was a young man willing to risk his remaining health based on nothing but anecdotes from strangers and scientific papers only peripherally related to his own condition. Here were dozens of others asking for information about how and where to sign up. Here was a medical doctor selling an untested treatment to desperate people — a treatment that would have been forbidden in the patient's own country.

As I read through the hundreds of posts that told this unfolding story, the image that came to mind was of a giant blackjack table. The players were holding their cards and placing their bets. The dealers were scooping up chips and shuffling the decks. The air had that kind of crazy hope and tension that comes with the possibility of a big fat payoff or a horrible loss. And a lot of the players were wearing blindfolds.

There were professional players — the scientists — who were counting cards and trying to beat the house. There were bankers deciding on who seemed likeliest to win. There were dealers who might or might not be cheating. There were many, many people in chairs who were clutching their chips and trying desperately to figure out how to play. Some, like the young man I just mentioned, had already put their money down. Some were feeling around for more information. And some were pushing back from the table, believing that there was no point in playing at all.

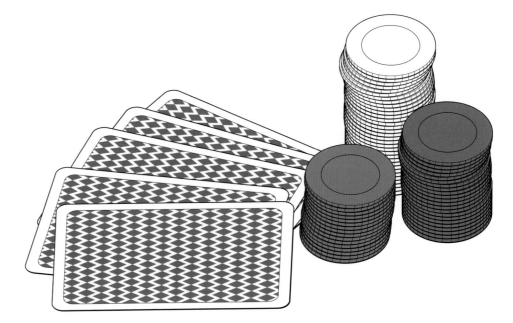

And so I decided to start with the chapters you've already seen, which you can think about this way: *Here are the four suits. Here are the colors of the cards. Here are three kinds of cells that function and interact in very specific ways.*

What's coming next is a look at how the larger game works, along with a close examination of what "winning" means for everybody at this table. For us, it means restoration of function. We want working fingers. We want to pee in the usual way. We want to have sex. We want to stand up. We want to breathe without ventilators.

But what is winning for a scientist? For the university that houses that scientist? What is it for investors? Where is big pharma in this picture? What is winning for the government? How about for insurance companies? What are the rules of this game, and who wrote them? Can the rules be changed? What happens when any of the players try to cheat?

That's the framework for the pages that follow. We're going to get outside this casino and understand, if we can, how it works *as a whole*. We're going to remove our blindfolds.

Part Two

Guests at the Party

6 CAN WE HELP?

Have you ever blundered into a conversation? You're at some kind of social event, maybe, where people who know each other well are talking amongst themselves. The subject seems familiar. You wade bravely in.

And what follows is a horrible awkward pause while the people all turn toward you with looks of puzzlement. They sip their drinks, waiting, eyebrows politely raised. You can't tell what's wrong with what you've said. Maybe you can correct the mistake if you listen for a bit. Maybe you'll find a way to fit in and say something useful. Maybe you'll just stand there for a moment and then fade away to join some other group.

That scene is how I picture what might happen if cells that aren't native to your spinal cord get dropped into it. They're guests at a loud and crowded party, trying to join an ongoing conversation. As we just learned, the normal healthy cord is made of only a few kinds of cells, and each of them has a very particular role to play in how the cord functions. What happens when an unfamiliar creature arrives and tries to join in?

For us, this is an important question because introducing new *kinds* of cells to the spinal cord is one approach that some scientists believe holds promise. Big promise. We're going to focus on two of those kinds of cells, both of which have already been put into many, many damaged spinal cords.

Before we get to them, though, we have to ask: *Why would anybody think of doing this?* What makes scientists believe that a cell that *isn't* a neuron, an astrocyte, or an oligodendrocyte would be welcome in the spinal cord, and what makes them think it would know what to do once it got there? A neural network isn't the sort of dance that just anybody can join.

The cells at the tips of the branches are all busy

The answer has to do with that development tree. You aren't going to find any of the cells at the tips of those branches just hanging around in your body with nothing to do. The central nervous system is in place, and all the cells that form it have jobs already. There's no spare-parts warehouse anywhere.

But, what if you could find a cell that hadn't yet made up its mind? Something a little further down the tree towards the main trunk; this is what scientists are after. They've been searching everywhere for a cell like that, hopefully somewhere in your own body… a cell that could be coaxed into turning itself into one of the cell types we need. Enter the *Mesenchymal (mez-zenKIME-ul) Stem Cell (MSC)*.

Suppose there was a population of cells hidden in your body that *could* become neurons if given the right kind of coaching and support. This would be fantastic news, because cells from your own body are already way ahead of cells from any other creature just in terms of safety.

Your body would be able to recognize them. Your immune system wouldn't attack them. You'd still have to figure out how to get them where you want them and then how to help them enter the "conversation" inside the cord, but it would be a start just to have them.

The word **chyme (KIME)** originally meant, basically, **glop**. It's liquid stuff. **Mesenchyme** is liquid stuff found in every new embryo. It's very special liquid stuff, though — heavily involved in the process by which the original identical cells that were a very early version of you transitioned to become almost every organ in your body.

It turns out that MSCs are at least a candidate to be that kind of cell. Very tiny collections of them exist in all of us, squirreled away in the marrow of our bones (called Marrow Stromal Cells in that case), in our fat, and even in some of our muscles. They're also found in the blood that flows through every human umbilical cord.

MSC's taken from umbilical cord blood are the most primitive, meaning that they're the furthest down the development trunk and therefore the ones with the most options still available to them. And that's why some scientists have spent years and years in their labs trying to see what would happen if these kinds of cells were transplanted into the damaged spinal cords of lab rats.

So, how is that working out?

How a stem cell qualifies as a stem cell

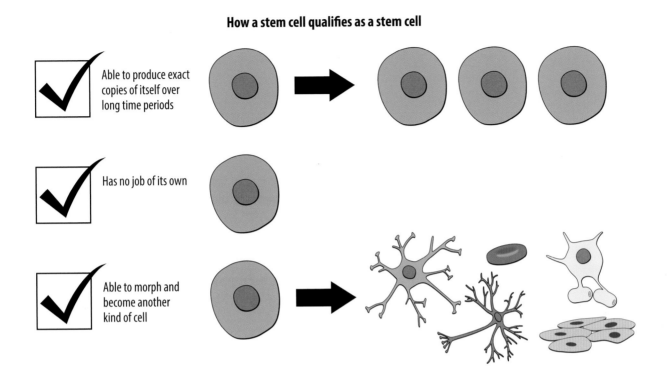

☑ Able to produce exact copies of itself over long time periods

☑ Has no job of its own

☑ Able to morph and become another kind of cell

So far, not as well as we'd like. These cells don't seem to be easy to turn into neurons. Or astrocytes. Or oligodendrocytes. There have been some labs that succeeded in coaxing their MSCs to look like neurons, but when those new cells were dropped into damaged rat spinal cords there wasn't much measurable recovery. Very sketchy evidence of new muscles firing. Hard to measure improvement in sensation. That doesn't mean it's impossible, but it hasn't happened yet.

In spite of that, there are some clinics around the world where these cells are being tested in people. An easy way to find out where is to visit the US government's webpage that shows what is being studied. All you have to do is type *clinicaltrials.gov* into your search engine, and the main page will pop up. After that you search the site using the combination *Mesenchymal Stem Cells + Spinal Cord Injury* to find out who might be working on this project right now. This is what I found in October of 2014:

There are fourteen studies listed.

- Of those studies, three have "Unknown" status, meaning that they haven't been updated in more than two years. They're probably dead.
- Of the remaining eleven, three are listed as "Complete," meaning (duh) that they're finished. If you come across a completed study that hasn't published its results, you can be pretty sure whatever they were trying didn't work the way they thought it would. None of the completed studies have posted results.
- Of the remaining eight, one has been suspended due to lack of funding. (Funding is a huge problem for this kind of work, as we'll see when we get to the section about money.)

> What is a clinical trial, anyway? It's a process. Volunteers sign up to get a specific intervention in a specific way. Then they're all carefully tested to see what effect the intervention had. Was it safe? Did anything change for the better? For the worse? Clinical trials are how drugs get approved so that you and I can buy them. They're how insurance companies decide what they'll cover and what they won't.

That leaves seven current clinical trials where MSCs are being tested in people with spinal cord injuries. All of them are either recruiting or planning to. As of 2014, one was in Chile, two were in South Korea, one was in Brazil, two were in Panama, and one was in Spain.

This is as good a place as any to talk about how on earth you'd decide to sign up for a clinical trial. I'm not talking about going overseas to pay someone for a treatment here — that's another subject that we'll be getting to shortly. This is about whether or not it makes sense for you to raise your hand to be included in a study.

As it happens, I know somebody who did that. His name is Bruce Hanson, and he's my husband.

He has a C6 injury that has turned out to be very incomplete. When he was about two years post, I was writing a book about how it is for a family to live through the first year after paralysis. Each of the chapters begins with a little quote, and I was looking for something to put at the front of the chapter where I describe us learning that he had a particular kind of damage to his cord. It's called Brown-Sequard Syndrome, and it involves an injury that's mostly confined to half the cord. In his case, the left side of his cord at C6 was pretty much toast, but the right half was more or less okay.

What that means in terms of function is that he has a lot of working muscles on his left side but hardly any on his right. At that point — after a ton of physical therapy — he was able to get up with a walker and kind of lurch around behind it. Anyway, I was trying to find a nice, juicy quote about Brown-Sequard, and I ran across this notice that patients with that kind of injury were being recruited for a study to help them walk, or walk better.

Whoa.

I went to the description of the trial. The people running it seemed legit. How could I tell? Because I looked up the name of the woman who was in charge; I read her resume and checked to see that she really was employed by a university and that she really did have experience in this field. I found the papers she had published and read them. So that's the very first thing to think about: Who is doing this? What was their training? What else have they done? Are they trustworthy? Are there any articles that question their integrity or qualifications? Is there reason to think the treatment might actually work?

In our case, the doctor's name was Andrea Behrman. She was legit. And the argument for her study seemed logical.

Next was to make sure Bruce fit the criteria for the kind of patient they were looking for. Age, gender, type of injury, time since injury, and other health issues are the sorts of things you'll find on these lists. He met all of them; he was a candidate.

Then we had to understand the potential downsides. Could the study hurt him in some way? Was he physically up to what would be required of him? Would being in this project disqualify him from being in some future one that might be better? Where would he need to be in order to participate, and for how long?

These are not small things. This study was a meticulous test of how much his ability to walk might be improved by 10 weeks of training. He would be suspended over a moving treadmill, and the researchers would place his right foot over and over onto the mat as it rolled underneath him.

He would need stamina and focus. He would need to be able to live alone and get himself to and from the lab every day for months, because we had young daughters who needed me at home with them. The lab was in Florida. Our house was near Seattle. If he was going to try to get in to the study, he needed to be serious; there's no point wasting the time and resources of researchers if you aren't pretty sure you can get all the way through the project. When people sign up and then drop out part way through, the scientists have nothing to show for their work and all of us lose.

So that was the second thing: Was he the right sort of person to do this? It would be intense, but he wanted to try. There seemed no reason not to, and so he applied and was accepted. I'm not sure how many research papers Dr. Behrman and her associates eventually got from the work she did with Bruce and others that year. I do know that those papers and that work have fed directly into our wider understanding of how to help people recover mobility once they have some signal in the cord. And that's crucial information for all of us.

What about Bruce? He spent a few months in Gainesville and came home using only a cane. This is called luck, I think. The combination of chance and very hard work.

I bring it up here because that gait-training trial is an example of a very low risk study and we were looking at what kinds of studies are currently going on in the Mesenchymal Stem Cell world. The same kinds of questions that Bruce and I asked would apply for someone considering taking part in one of those.

Are the researchers legit? Is there reason to believe that the cells would help and do no harm? What exactly is involved in being a participant? Would a person who got these cells still be able to enroll in a different study later? MSCs, remember, are not native to the spinal cord. Is there maybe another kind of cell that might work better?

On to our next guest at the party.

7 BACK AT THE PARTY

Okay, so maybe those Mesenchymal Stem Cells aren't all that good at joining the spinal cord conversation. They seem to need too much grooming and training, which makes sense because they're not native speakers of the language that neurons, astrocytes, and oligodendrocytes share. There's some evidence, though, that MSCs might function — in terms of this analogy — sort of like mute caterers.

That's to say, even though they don't easily hang out and chat with the partygoers, they do seem able to deliver a form of nourishment. When MSCs have been placed into damaged animal spinal cords, they secrete little doses of what scientists call "growth factors." That sounds important, right? If we ever find a way to deliver real replacement cells, we need those replacements to thrive, grow, and do their jobs. Growth factors would definitely be invited to that party. They wouldn't have to say a word.

Are there any other cells already in the body that might be better replacement cell candidates?

As it turns out, yes. They're called *Olfactory Ensheathing Cells (OECs)*. Before we get to how they might be used in repairing a busted spinal cord, let's have a look at their normal lives. The word, *olfactory*, is a clue here.

Olfactory means "having to do with your sense of smell." An olfactory cell is one that's involved in you being able to tell the difference between a blooming lilac and a wet Golden Retriever, with your eyes closed and your hands in your lap and your ears plugged.

The reason you can do that is because a patch of flesh on the inside of your nose is lined with

It would be so helpful if scientists could settle on a single name for things! Here are some names you might run across for these cells:

- Olfactory Ensheathing Cells (OEC)
- Olfactory Ensheathing Glia (OEG)
- Olfactory Ensheathing Glial Cells (also OEG)
- Olfactory Schwann Cells (not usually given an acronym)

47

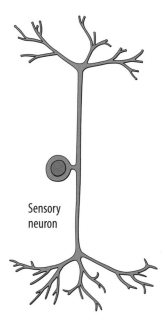

Sensory
neuron

the "listening" ends of sensory neurons — yes, exactly the same kind of cells that deliver the "ouch" when you've stepped on a nail. The ones that drive your sense of smell are called Olfactory Neurons. They have that familiar sensory cell-type body with its two axons going off in opposite directions.

Here's what smelling actually is.

First, there are molecules floating in the air. They're released, say, by a chocolate cake in the oven. The molecules wander up through your nostrils and drift back into the open space behind your nose, which is called the nasal cavity. The receptor ends of your 12 million Olfactory Neurons are there, buried just below the surface, waiting. The surface the molecules are headed for is called the Olfactory Epithilium; its total area is a little bigger than the top of a US quarter.

Each of those receptors is keyed to recognize *a single one* of the thousands of kinds of floating odor molecules. (This kind of fact is why I love neuroscience… your nose and mine have cells that can distinguish between types of red wine.)

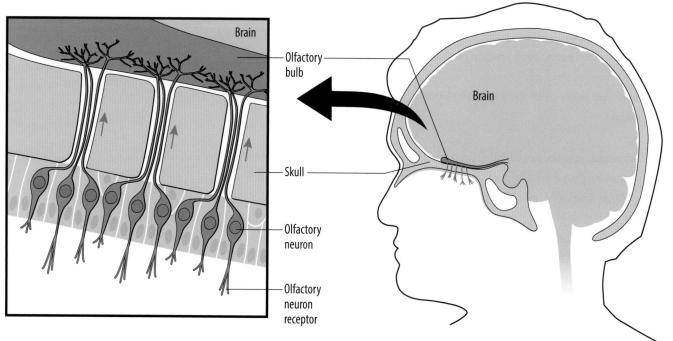

When the receptor on the receiving end of an Olfactory Neuron senses its special molecule, a message zips up its axon, races through the cell body, and shoots onto the other end of the neuron, which is sitting inside your skull in a bit of tissue that's part of your brain. That bit of tissue is called the Olfactory Bulb. The bulb, in turn, is connected by more neurons to areas of your brain that can learn and remember what chocolate cake smells like. Stay with me, here. There's a reason we need to understand a little about the mechanics of this system.

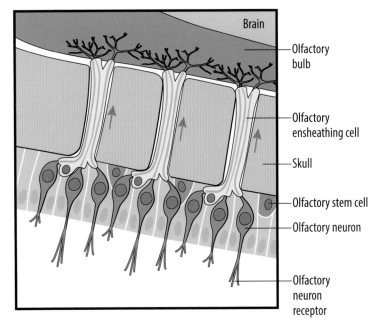

The whole sense-of-smell thing must be extremely important in terms of keeping our species alive, because those Olfactory Neurons are unique among all the other neurons in our brains and spinal cords. How so? *They regenerate. When one of them quits functioning or dies off, it gets replaced.* In fact, those neurons are constantly being replaced all your life; the entire Olfactory Epithilium gets remade once or twice a month. Apparently, stone-age humans needed their sense of smell to stay sharp.

So what we know is that there's a kind of sensory neuron that our bodies can replace. And if a neuron can be replaced, there must be primitive cells nearby that know how to become olfactory neurons. *There must be a supply of stem cells.* And it turns out that's exactly right.

That surface called the Olfactory Epithilium has a whole layer made of stem cells. Those stem cells make it possible for your body to replace these — and only these — neurons. But that's not all. It wouldn't do much good if the new crop of neurons lacked the kind of insulation that makes it possible for signals to travel along their axons. If the olfactory stem cells created only olfactory neurons, the system would break down. They have to be able to create some "wrapper" cells, too.

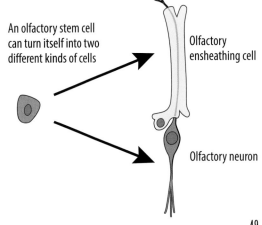

An olfactory stem cell can turn itself into two different kinds of cells

And they do. Olfactory stem cells can turn themselves into two different kinds of cells: olfactory neurons and olfactory ensheathing cells (OECs) — which brings us, finally, back where we started in this chapter. It's the wrapper cells, which we're going to call OECs. Our second candidate for a new guest at the party is not a stem cell at all. It's one of the two kinds of cells that are *created by* those very special stem cells inside your nose.

Remember Schwann cells? Back when we were talking about the wrapper cells that make axons in your arms and legs work properly, I said this:

> *When the axons they've wrapped themselves around get damaged, Schwann cells don't just give up and wither away, like oligodendrocytes do in the spinal cord. Instead, they do this amazing transformer thing, where instead of clinging desperately to the dying axon, they re-shape themselves to form a sort of tunnel. The tunnel is a surface for the broken stub of the axon to travel along, aiming straight at the old target muscle. Inside the tunnel they've built, the Schwann cells are also pumping out growth factors — molecules that are like vitamins to the axon... Once the axon is safely growing toward its muscle, the Schwann cell turns back into a wrapper so that signals can travel.*

Scientists figured out about 15 years ago that those OECs might be able to help out a damaged spinal cord, and ever since they've been trying every which way to make that happen. They're not trying to make the nose *neurons* work in the cord; instead, they're trying to see if the *wrapper cells* designed for those neurons can give a boost to surviving axons in a busted cord. This seems not too crazy, because remember, your OECs are partly in your nose and partly in your brain. They're the only cells that seem at home in both the peripheral nervous system *and* the central nervous system. That's worth at least an invitation to the party.

What happened in 2000 is that a neuroscientist in Madrid published a really shocking paper about her work with OECs and lab rats. Her name is Dr. Almudena Ramon-Cueta. The paper said, basically, that OECs worked. She had cut right through the cords of her rats and given them transplants of OECs. After a few months those rats were walking. If it worked in people the same way, it was going to be a cure.

Which is why, when doctors in Portugal and China offered their own versions of that treatment to anybody who met their criteria and could pay, thousands of people with spinal cord injuries took them up on it. These weren't clinical trials. They were untested-in-humans treatments, with no guarantees of anything.

When Bruce and I were very new to this strange new world of paralysis, we could barely figure out how to keep our clothes right-side out. Every bloody thing was hard: sleeping, waking up, eating, using a toilet, driving, thinking, talking. It was all hard. We had no time or energy to think about science or cures.

At some point, though, we got the hang of what the shrinks call "the new normal."

You all know what I mean by this… the day you realize that you're not *completely* frustrated, afraid, exhausted, and defeated. You're coping. When those kinds of days started piling up for us, we did begin to wonder about where the science was. Any hope out there at all? And that's how we first heard of OECs and the possibility that they might help cure paralysis. We didn't have to look far, because OECs were in the news quite a lot back then.

It was the summer of 2003.

The story I remember most clearly was about a woman named Susan Fajt (pronounced *FATE*). She was a beautiful blonde; picture the bright, animated women who deliver the news on some cable channels. I saw her image online — a lovely 24-year-old with a very severe injury in the middle of her back and a determination to get well as quickly as possible, no matter what it took. Like my husband, she had been injured in 2001, and also like him, she had struggled for months just to stay alive.

When I first heard of Susan, she was describing her recent trip to Lisbon, Portugal, where a doctor named Carlos Lima had operated on her. The surgery had two parts. One doctor — an ear, nose, and throat specialist — took a small amount of tissue from the back of her nasal cavity. His job was to collect a bit of the olfactory epithilium. Dr. Lima then opened her back, exposed the damaged place in her spinal cord, and placed a tiny, carefully chopped up blob of the harvested epithilium material directly into the site of her injury. Then he closed

> In November of 2003, **The New Yorker** had this to report about Dr. Hongyun Huang of Beijing:
>
> Since news of Huang's success leaked out on Internet discussion groups, thousands of desperate patients have contacted him. Huang has set up a program that allows Americans and other non-Chinese to visit Beijing for one month, for surgery and preliminary rehabilitation. The cost is twenty thousand dollars; six thousand people, Huang says, are now on a waiting list for the program.

her up. The tissue wasn't processed or cultured at all; there was no attempt to sort out the mucus cells from the olfactory neuron cell bodies from the OECs from the stem cells. It was literally a stew of all these things. The price of this procedure was $27,000, not including travel to and from Lisbon.

Susan reported back to one of the first internet sites for people with spinal cord injuries (CareCure) on July 5, 2003:

> *I am the third patient out of the USA to recieve his procedure!! It has been 12 days since the day of surgery and I recovered some sensation within the first couple of days… feel very hopeful for the future.*

That post (and others like it from Dr. Huang's lab in China) electrified the community. No one in the USA was putting cells of any kind into us! There were no clinical trials of OECs, and there was no legal way to get this done here. It seemed like a perfect example of how our entrenched and over-regulated bureaucracy was costing us our chance at getting better.

What developed over the next year was a different, and sadder story.

8 Both Ends of the Spectrum

Susan Fajt didn't get what she wanted from her transplant.

I followed her tragedy as it unfolded online over the next few years, though at first it wasn't obvious what was going on. That's because it was hard to tell exactly how her body was responding to the surgery. Like Susan herself, we all wanted so much to believe in these cells, and every little tweak and twitch seemed like a good sign. The cells had worked on rats, right? That seemed reason enough to start operating on people; there was cheering for the idea that somebody was finally going to stop messing around watching rats get better. A few weeks after Dr. Lima's procedure, Susan told us this:

> *i still feel that i have made the right decision in regards to my surgery. Bladder control is still better, and some other interesting things seem to be going on in my body, i will post them as soon as it is verified by tests. There does seem to be more pain and spasticity, though it could be a sign that signals are getting through to the desired location!!*

Actually as it turned out, the cells had **not** worked reliably in rats. No scientists had managed to get the kind of spectacular results that Dr. Almudena Ramon-Cueta had described in her paper back in 2000, and not for lack of trying. They just couldn't do it.

Wait. *There does seem to be more pain and spasticity?* Uh oh. That sentence was like an alarm going off on my computer screen — a blinking icon shaped like a storm cloud. And we later found out that the bladder "control" she referred to wasn't control — it was a faint warning, sometimes, that she might need to cath. In the meantime, she got no voluntary movement of any muscles in her legs. They were as dead as ever, except when they were going rigid with new spasms. And she was in pain.

After another month, she was still hoping for the best.

My legs are so much stronger that they are giving me a good fight! I don't know exactly what this means, however i do know that it makes me have to stretch often and standing is a must. Perhaps this is my bodies way of telling me to get up and moving or else it will punish me by cramping up and hurting.. I also have small spasms that lead me to believe that signals are moving to the legs giving me hope for more coordinated return in the future.

I read those lines today and imagine her struggling to get control of her legs, trying to do some kind of workout or just haul herself safely into her standing frame while her thighs were going rigid with spasms. She was — at least online — still upbeat, dealing with it and staying positive. That slowly changed.

In case you're really lucky and missed the whole stem cell debate that wasted so much time back around 2001-2008, here's the deal: One way to sort stem cells is by looking at what stage of life they're present in. Embryonic stem cells are present only in embryos. Fetal stem cells are only in fetuses. And adult stem cells are only in us after we're born. The OECs that were supposed to help Susan were **none of the above.**

A year after her surgery, Susan appeared on television, giving bizarre testimony to a subcommittee of the US Senate. The politicians were quite obviously interested in using her as a campaign prop, asking solicitous questions about her "amazing recovery" as they nodded at one another over how miraculous these "adult stem cells" were. A google search today on her name + adult stem cells returns more than 30,000 places to read about how she was cured.

She wasn't cured, of course. About four years after her surgery she stopped making public comments at all, but she did confide the truth to a few close friends: she'd gained *nothing* from the procedure. Susan died of an apparent drug overdose at the age of 32 in January of 2010.

I'm guessing that in spite of stories like Susan's, at least some of you are thinking about the idea of spending upwards of $30,000 in cash to have a surgery that might help you, might hurt you, might do nothing at all for you.

I understand that, because we did. We thought about it.

We thought about it a lot, especially when we read that the sooner you got this sort of surgery after injury, the more likely it was to work. It was like, the window was closing fast, and every day of not doing something might mean less chance of getting better. That was the decision Susan Fajt made: she thought that she couldn't afford to wait.

Dr. Lima, for his part, made a decision to go directly to human patients without waiting for more rat studies; he published his results on his first seven patients in 2006. If you picture a line with the most cautious researchers at the far left and the least cautious at the far right, Dr. Lima was way out there at the right edge of the page. At the other end, there were many, many scientists who kept plugging away with rat studies, trying to build up a body of knowledge so that if they ever got to a place where they could test OECs in people, they'd be certain of doing — at the very least — no harm.

The question we started with was this: *Could OECs be helpful in repairing a damaged spinal cord? Are these cells likely to be able to fit in and play nicely with cells that live there naturally?* It seems obvious that if you wanted to answer that question, you'd need to figure out how to isolate those OECs. Remember that the reason we think they might work is that their regular job is to create a runway — a path — on which your smelling neuron axons can grow out of your nose and up into your brain. Axons need a runway if they're going to grow, they're just fussy that way. And if OECs already know how to survive inside the brain, they might do okay in the spinal cord, too. Both are part of the central nervous system.

If you scraped some tissue out of the Olfactory Epithelium, you'd want to sort it out before you put it into somebody's spinal cord.

What would you expect to find in your little blob of tissue? It would be a mix of the things pictured at the right. What Dr. Lima did was to take a sharp knife, chop up the blob, mix the pieces with a little spinal fluid, and put the whole mess into the injury site. Within a few hours, the entire procedure was done. What about the cautious scientists at the other end of the line?

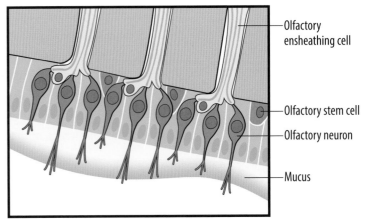

Olfactory ensheathing cell

Olfactory stem cell

Olfactory neuron

Mucus

Just about the time Susan Fajt was making her way to Lisbon to have her surgery, a group of very cautious scientists working out of Griffith University in Queensland, Australia, had decided they knew enough about how to sort the blob to run a very small, very carefully controlled trial. They started by looking for participants. Here's how they described that process in the paper they published later:

> *… it was considered important that serious attempts were made to ensure that the participants were able to comprehend fully the potential benefits (or lack of benefit) and risks associated with the procedure. In other words, that the participants had the personal psychological strength to deal with any outcome …*

In plainer language, they needed to be sure that their patients could take whatever happened. Here's how serious they were about that: they took two full years to find just six people who met their very exacting standards for psychological health. They actually had been hoping to have a few more people in the trial, but decided to go with six because they didn't want to invest any more time in looking. Their list of criteria included:

- Emotional stability
- Realistic expectations
- Stable family situation
- Lack of drug dependence
- Lack of alcohol dependence

Because this was a controlled and authorized clinical trial, none of the participants paid anything to be enrolled.

I can't even begin to do justice to the process this team used to separate the precious OECs from the rest of the tissue taken from these patients' noses. If you picture a well-equipped chemistry lab with about 30 consecutive workstations, you begin to get an idea of how it worked. Start by putting a tiny camera into the nasal cavity. Then use a pair of sterile forceps to collect five tiny blobs of tissue. Store the blobs on a sterile culture and bathe them in antibiotics. Keep them cold. After that, continue the sorting through a meticulous protocol that goes on for *four weeks*, until there's absolute certainty that the OECs are pure.

At that point the volunteer patient comes back to the hospital; it's time for the second part of the surgery. The doctors expose the damaged cord and inject those oh-so-carefully harvested cells into it. They use their super-calibrated machines to create a grid pattern of injections in the damaged area itself and a short distance above and below it. The needles are 362 micrometers wide — about as wide as a bundle of three or four average human hairs.

So. Spend two years finding six qualified patients. Collect nasal tissue, sort and purify OECs, inject several million of them into the damaged cords, close the patients' backs up again … and wait. Because this was what they call a safety study, there was zero expectation that these patients would recover any sensation or movement as a result. Zero. The researchers purposefully used only a tiny fraction of the number of cells they thought the patients would need for recovery.

The whole point — the long years of animal testing, the careful selection of patients, the meticulous surgery — was just to test the procedure. Is it really possible to get pure and healthy OECs safely out of noses and into living human beings? If they did, would the patients suffer any bad outcomes as a result?

There were no bad outcomes in the Australian trial. None of the patients had more pain, and none of them experienced more spasticity. They also didn't recover any sensation or movement, which was expected given the tiny dose of OECs injected into their spines. The research could continue. Pure OECs were safe.

> It helps me to think of safety studies as tiny tastes of some new food. You take a little bit on your tongue to see if you like it. You don't expect to feel satisfied after that, but you do expect to know if the new food is any good. That's what safety studies are: tiny tastes of therapies that might turn out to be terrific.

In June of 2014, a troubling news report underlined the need for safety and caution. One of Dr. Lima's early patients had shown up at her local hospital with serious pain in her back. Injured at age 18, she'd gone to Lisbon in the hope that his procedure would help her recover some kind of sensation or even movement. Instead, she got nothing. During the eight years between the time of her transplant and the pain that sent her to the hospital, though, the cell concoction Lima had put into her injury site had been alive and working on its own agenda.

When surgeons opened her back and exposed her injury/transplant site, they found a mess of nasal tissue that was secreting mucus — ordinary *snot* — inside her spinal cord. The olfactory mucosa mash-up was, at least in her case, a catastrophe.

In October 2014, news broke that a transplant of OECs had given a Polish man back the ability to walk. Video of him taking painful steps along a wooden bridge, unassisted, flashed into my own mailbox from dozens of friends. He was leaning heavily on a sturdy walker and using what appeared to be elastic bands to get his legs to move forward. Was this going to be Susan Fajt all over again? Could we trust that this time, something real had happened?

Darek Fidyka was a fireman when he was attacked in the summer of 2010 by a murderously jealous husband. The stab wound that paralyzed Darek created a complete gap in his cord — a hole about half the radius of a US dime. That's a lot of missing axons. Like so many people confronting life in a wheelchair, he went to work on an aggressive rehab program. For more than a year, he pushed himself through a rigorous physical therapy routine, but saw no improvement. When he was chosen to be in the OEC study, the first thing that happened was *another* eight months of aggressive rehab, this time supervised by the researchers.

Why? Because the scientist running this study, Dr. Geoffrey Raisman, wanted to make sure that if there was any recovery it would be the result of the cells and not just something that would have happened anyway if Darek tried harder. At the end of what was then twenty-one straight months of effort with no measurable results, a team of Polish doctors did the transplant.

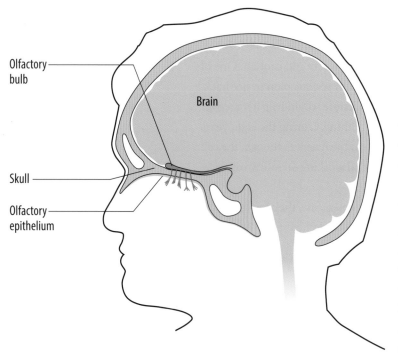

Olfactory bulb

Brain

Skull

Olfactory epithelium

This time, there was no mucosa mash-up; in fact, the cells that went into Darek's injury site came originally not from the Olfactory Epithilium, but from the other end of the OECs inside his skull. These doctors completely removed one of his two olfactory bulbs. They used it to culture OECs in a process similar to what the Australian scientists had developed — a weeks-long effort that resulted in pure OECs, ready to transplant.

There was another wrinkle to the procedure Darek got, though. The surgeons didn't just inject his OECs into his cord; instead, they harvested four tiny strips of nerve tissue (meaning, bundles of axons) from one of his ankles. Those four strips were placed across the hole in his cord, where they would hopefully form a sort of bridge upon which the OECs could guide the axons to grow. That was the idea.

Six difficult months later, Darek could take steps with help from a PT while wearing leg braces. Two years after that, he became the face of possibility for injured people all around the world. There are still many doubters, but Dr. Raisman isn't among them. Seeing Darek's recovery after spending more than 30 years in careful research with OECs, he had this to say:

> *What we've done is establish a principle — nerve fibres can grow back and restore function, provided we give them a bridge. To me, this is more impressive than a man walking on the Moon. I believe this is the moment when paralysis can be reversed.*

9   Schwann Cells Redux

This party is getting crowded! Now seems like a good time to take a breath and recall what exactly is the problem we're trying to solve. A healthy cord is made of just three kinds of cells: neurons, oligodendrocytes, and astrocytes. Neurons are cell bodies with long, long threads attached to them; the threads are called axons. Neurons are the oh-so-critical carriers of information to and from the brain. Oligodendrocytes are responsible for creating this stuff called *myelin*, which coats the axons in such a way that they can transmit specific messages at warp speed in a network of millions of neurons. Astrocytes are there to do basic management and maintenance work; they keep the whole system running smoothly.

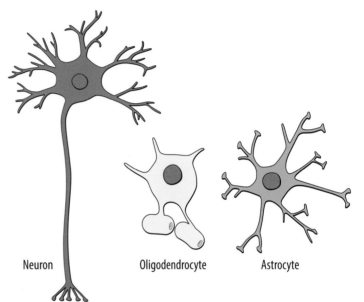

Neuron   Oligodendrocyte   Astrocyte

A damaged cord has a scar created by the astrocytes and a bunch of ruptured axons that can't grow through that scar even if they wanted to. That's the scene.

The issue we need to resolve is this: the central nervous system as a whole was never meant to repair itself. There are no instructions written into these three kinds of cells that would allow them to re-group and get back to work after a catastrophe. What we're after in this part of the book is an answer to the question of whether it might be possible for some other kind of cell to help out.

If you're like me, there comes a point when it's too hard to keep all the information straight without some kind of guide. Here's my attempt at capturing where we are right now, along with hints at where we're headed.

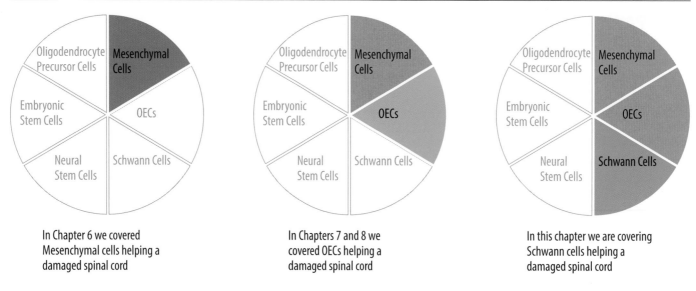

In Chapter 6 we covered Mesenchymal cells helping a damaged spinal cord

In Chapters 7 and 8 we covered OECs helping a damaged spinal cord

In this chapter we are covering Schwann cells helping a damaged spinal cord

The first couple of wedges represent the kinds of cells we just covered: Mesenchymal cells and OECs. We've already spent a little time talking about the third wedge, which is the Schwann cells. What follows is both a reminder and an update.

You have axons both inside and outside your central nervous system, and all of them need to be wrapped in myelin. Outside your cord, the cells that make myelin are Schwann cells; they're the wrapper cells for all the axons in your peripheral nervous system. The best thing about Schwann cells, from our perspective, is that they don't dry up when you need them most — after an injury.

Suppose a healthy person with a fully functioning nervous system gets into a minor car crash — a fender bender. Suppose also that this person has something sharp on the seat next to her that's not tied down; it could be a tool or anything made of metal. If she's going 25 mph and her car is hit in such a way that it stops very suddenly, the sharp metal object might just fly into her shin at 25 mph. *Ouch.* She's likely to have damage not just to the muscles in that shin, but also to the bundles of axons — the *nerves* — that connect to those muscles.

What happens as she recovers is that the Schwann cells do the transformer thing I described earlier: they morph into little runways and secrete nutritious molecules. The broken axons settle onto the runways, eat up the molecules, grow back, and reattach to the muscles. The

Schwann cells then revert to their normal job of wrapping the axons in myelin. The unlucky driver does a lot of physical therapy and, after a time, things mostly work as they did before.

We care about this because if Schwann cells could be persuaded to do this trick not just inside a person's shin but also deep inside her spinal cord, we might have a way to get axons to pass through an injury site. People have been working on this possibility in rats for decades. Thousands and thousands of rats have been used to create a body of evidence that points toward Schwann cells as good candidates for being very special guests at our party.

That's the refresher. Now for the update.

Down in the very southeastern corner of the USA there's an institution called The Miami Project. It's housed on the campus of the University of Miami, where it's an important part of the Miller School of Medicine. More than 300 people work there, all focused on one thing: finding a way to end paralysis.

It's taking a lot longer than anyone hoped. The name, The Miami Project, was chosen because the plan was to re-create some of the conditions that allowed a group of scientists to build the first atomic weapons. *The Manhattan Project* — so named because its head offices were in New York City — was a frantic, massive, well-funded, tightly coordinated effort to build an atomic bomb before the Nazis did. *The Miami Project* was meant to have that same sense of urgency. It would gather the most qualified people, provide them with necessary resources, and push on until a cure was delivered.

As we all know, that hasn't happened yet.

The Miami Project has, however, at long last managed to untangle the knots of issues around one particular therapy: how to use Schwann cells in human patients. In this country you can't test a new drug in human beings without first getting permission from the federal government. The Food and Drug Administration (FDA) is the "mother" in what sometimes looks from the outside like a painfully slow and elaborate game of Mother May I.

Nick Buoniconti was a spectacular linebacker for the Miami Dolphins during their championship seasons in 1973 and 1974. When his son, Marc, was paralyzed in a college football game 12 years later, Nick led the team that eventually formed the Miami Project. It's very common to find that the founders of major spinal cord injury research institutions are relatives of people with wealth or fame or both.

In that game, one player is the authority figure (mother) who repeatedly gives and denies permission for the others to move forward. She makes all the rules. She decides when each player has been sufficiently compliant. She decides when they must go back to the starting line. When the Miami Project scientists first submitted their written Schwann cell application to the FDA, it was 2007. That was the starting line.

At that point those scientists had been working with rat studies for decades and they believed they knew the answer to every conceivable question the FDA might have. They were wrong. Over the course of the next five years, they had to look at things they hadn't even dreamed would be issues.

How can you be sure that your cells aren't going to go wild and cause tumors to grow?

Look at all our evidence. We transplanted our cells into hundreds and hundreds of rats, and not one of them ever developed any sort of tumor.

Where did you look for those tumors?

At the site of the implants, of course.

You didn't consider that the cells could have migrated up or down the spinal cord and formed tumors some distance away from the original implants?

No...

Back to the starting line with you.

And so, back to the lab they went. Ordered more rats. Waited for them to arrive. Spent a week or so making sure they were comfortable and healthy. Did testing on each one to create a sort of baseline: *Rat #342 can navigate the horizontal ladder in 6.3 seconds without missing any rungs.* Gave the rats their injuries. Waited a week. Did the cell transplants. Waited two or three months. Repeated the original testing: *How is Rat #342 managing the horizontal ladder today? How does she compare to our control rat over here who has a similar injury but got no cells?* Sacrificed the rats. Put every micro-thin slice of their spinal cords through a battery of staining and tracing and analysis.

Don't mess up the recordkeeping. Above all, make sure your paperwork is in order. At one point during this long process, one of their hundreds of rats had died — and nobody had recorded what happened. Because the FDA is looking with a giant magnifying glass at every detail of every procedure, they naturally wanted to know what happened to that animal. It nearly derailed the whole deal.

When the Miami Project's final application was set on a table late in 2012, five years after they'd begun the process, it formed a stack of documents that was a foot high. It took another year for the FDA to say the magic words, *"You may."* The work to get to that moment had cost about $15 million, every dime of which came from grants, endowment interest, and fundraisers. By the summer of 2014 doctors had transplanted Schwann cells into their first three patients, all of whom were newly injured. In October of that same year the news got even better: they were going to try the cells in patients with chronic injuries.

What all of this means is that Schwann cells have been officially invited to the party, and some of them are already in the room. These first three cell candidates fall into the group of cells defined as *autologous* (aw-TALL-uh-guss). The word literally means *written by oneself*, which is accurate. All these cells come not from the donated tissue of others, but from us, from our own bodies.

The rest of the candidates are another story.

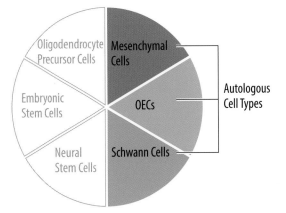

10 Visitors from Another Galaxy

Okay. We know now that there are a few cell types inside your own body that might be able to help restore some of what was lost when your cord got damaged. The great thing about these kinds of cells is that they're *you*; your immune system will recognize them as *you* and leave them alone.

The not-so-great thing is that we're asking them to do work they weren't designed for, and we want them to do that work in an unfamiliar environment. They're like Korean finish carpenters trying to repair broken plumbing in Hoboken. An OEC knows how to guide a sensory axon from inside your nose up into your brain. It knows how to provide a myelin coat for that axon. Does it follow that it will also be able to do that trick with every sensory axon inside your cord? How about the axons attached to brain neurons that eventually link to muscles? The answer at this point is a definite *maybe*.

There's one more problem to keep in mind, though, and that's the difficulty of making sure the cells taken from a person's body are pure. What scientists in Poland and Australia and Miami and elsewhere are doing is inventing elaborate processes that guarantee that the cells they intend to transplant will be immaculate. That takes equipment, expertise, and time. It isn't going to be something that happens in every hospital; there won't be batches of OECs or Schwann cells in little refrigerators waiting for new patients.

And that means — just being practical — that a treatment based on this kind of cell has to work spectacularly well in order to become standard. Let's look at the way people with multiple myeloma are treated to get an idea of how much work is ahead of us. Multiple myeloma is cancer of the blood. To treat it, doctors begin by collecting some of the patient's own bone marrow, extracting mesenchymal stem cells from it, and then purifying those cells. So far, that sounds a lot like what happened to the guy in Poland whose OECs were taken from his nasal cavity.

Then the multiple myeloma patients get radiation and chemotherapy, which makes them intensely sick for weeks. Then they get their own stem cells back. Then they wait for months while the stem cells replace the bone marrow that was killed off earlier.

And then they get better.

These treatments work, at least for a time. People who get them recover their health and live *years* longer than people who don't. That's a powerful reason why insurance companies are required to cover them. There's no system like that in place for us, at least not yet. No network of cell centers where we could go to have this kind of work done safely and reliably. No database to convince insurance regulators that this treatment is so effective that it deserves to be covered.

One interesting side note about that Polish patient: A scientist told me recently that from her perspective, the important part of his recovery wasn't that the OECs worked, but that they worked on a patient who was known to have **zero** connection through his damaged cord. She said that his recovery means that everyone needs to reconsider the very idea of a "complete" injury. **It's possible there's no such thing.**

All of that would need to be in place for us. I'm saying, if we're going to push for treatments that involve the cells on the right side of the circle, we have to look at the myeloma model to see how much needs to be done before it could work.

What about the left side?

The cells over there are not taken from the patients' own bodies. They start out somewhere else completely. They're visitors from another galaxy. That means — theoretically — that they *could* be produced in batches, stored in ordinary hospitals, and made available just as other drugs are.

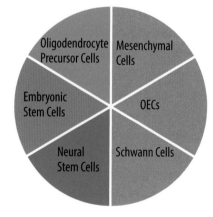

Remember that what we're after with these cell-based therapies is a way to *replace* the actual cells that were lost when the original injury happened. We might need some of everything — some neurons that can grow new axons to make new connections, some oligodendrocytes to make myelin coats for those axons, and some astrocytes to keep the system up and running. The problem is that there are no spares of these cell types in any adult bodies. Can we build spares?

Here's the tree again. The place where the big branch on the right splits off into neural stem cells and cells that will become eyes and skin is the place we're going to talk about now. During the early days of human development, the cells of an embryo are sorting themselves into groups. There's a brief period when there are no neurons, oligodendrocytes, or astrocytes… just neural stem cells. Those neural stem cells are like a set of specialized Legos that, once they've become locked into place, can't be unlocked. And the set is limited in both time and quantity. You only have so many, and they only exist for a short time.

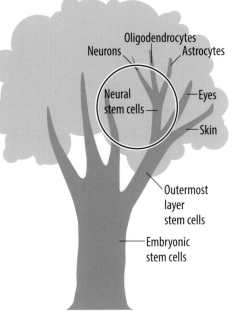

So, could we get hold of neural stem cells themselves? It seems at least possible that if we could, they'd go ahead and do what they're programmed to do: continue to grow and turn themselves into the basic elements of a working spinal cord. As it turns out, the time during a human fetus's development when there are neural stem cells present is between sixteen and twenty weeks post conception.

Yes. *Sixteen to twenty weeks.* This is only a month or two before a pregnancy becomes "viable." The earliest time for a premature infant to be born and have any chance to survive is about twenty-three weeks. So, are we talking about taking fetal cells? Cells from a miscarriage or even a planned abortion? There are people with chronic spinal cord injuries who are having neural stem cells implanted right now, in a pair of FDA-approved clinical trials. Did the cells they're being given originate in a sixteen-to-twenty-week human fetus?

They did. The companies that are running these trials have populations of human neural stem cells that are pure, safe, and sustainable. They came from fetal material, *in a single event.* There was a miscarriage or a planned abortion. The mother (or both parents) gave informed consent for the scientists to harvest neural stem cells if they could. And that miscarriage or planned abortion (I don't know which it was) happened a while ago, back in 1999.

That was the year that neural stem cells were first isolated and purified, by a woman working for a company called StemCells, Inc. The great thing about stem cells, remember, is that

The idea of using fetal cells to build sustainable cell lines is hardly new. Two lines of cells, called WI-38 and MRC-5, are the source of the **measles-mumps-rubella** vaccines commonly given to babies and young children. Both of these cell lines have been around for more than 50 years; both derive from two tiny bits of fetal tissue donated in the 1960s.

they can reproduce themselves indefinitely if you give them the right environment to do so. Once you've succeeded in gathering a blob of neural stem cells, you only have to tend that blob.

You have a stem cell *line*, and the descendants of that line will grow and replicate themselves in the lab, independently, for as long as we need them. Think of sourdough starter — the stuff that bakers used for centuries to get bread to rise before yeast was on every grocery shelf. I have a friend who bakes her bread using sourdough that is descended from a batch her great-grandmother used more than a century ago. Same idea as a stem cell line, but not well understood by the general public.

For example.

About ten years ago I was sitting in the bar at a local golf club, waiting for my teenaged daughter to finish her game so I could drive her home. Next to me was a group of men who looked to be in early retirement — bald, a little pouchy, not in any hurry. They were talking amongst themselves, and I was eavesdropping shamelessly. One of them was explaining in great detail about how stem cells work. While the others shook their heads in disgust, he described how the doctors grow the fetuses and infants to a certain point and then kill them to get their stem cells. He explained that it would be necessary to keep doing this every time you wanted to get more cells. It was about as horrifying as anything could ever be. He spoke with absolute certainty; I still have the page from my journal where I recorded this conversation as I listened.

A couple of years later there was a best-selling novel about a boarding school for young people who seemed normal but were actually clones of regular kids. Their only purpose in life was to stay healthy so they could give up their body parts for their matches in the ordinary world. That novel (*Never Let Me Go*) was nominated for many major fiction prizes. It was made into a film. It was also, to me, another version of the crazy talk I'd overheard in the golf club bar. When it came to the idea of stem cells and cloning, there was genuine fear and horror during the years around the turn of the 21st century.

Here's the reality about how fetal-derived neural stem cells have been studied and used to try to repair damaged spinal cords. 1999 was the breakthrough year, the year we first had a real collection of human neural stem cells to work with. That collection became a *line*, just like the lines of fetal cells that have been producing vaccines for decades. The old golfer's ugly fantasy about growing baby after baby to get their cells is ridiculous; his certainty that it was real is what's troubling.

Between 1999 and 2011, scientists at university labs and in biotech startups struggled to test neural stem cells on animals — mostly mice and rats. Twelve years of repeating experiments under different conditions. Twelve years of submitting their papers for review. Twelve years of publications and reworking of theories and trying again. Twelve years of looking for tumors. Twelve years of seeing rats and mice recover function.

In 2011, StemCells, Inc. began at long last to inject their neural stem cells into their first three human patients. All three were young men, and all three had complete, chronic spinal cord injuries — meaning that they'd had zero sensation or movement since they got hurt. Each guy got a tiny dose of cells, calibrated to be big enough to do some damage (if that's what was going to happen), but not big enough to do any good. The surgeries were done in Zurich, Switzerland, because the doctors there had created some unbelievably finely tuned instruments to measure changes in the central nervous system.

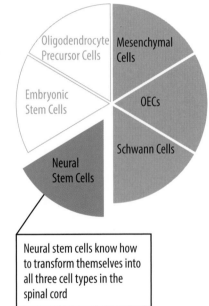

Neural stem cells know how to transform themselves into all three cell types in the spinal cord

Recently I got to talk with one of the patients who went to Zurich for the StemCells, Inc. treatment. His name is Lee Thibeault.

> *The biggest thing to participate in the study, honestly, is having the mindset for it. And my mindset was believing that this would be beneficial for myself and beneficial for others to move the progress forward.*

> *I'm not going to say that it was anything pleasant to be bedridden on my back for six to seven days after the surgery, the transplant, to allow for the dura to seal up watertight, and then to get back into my chair and suffer from that much muscle atrophy after being in bed for that many days. And now to show up every three months and have them put pins and needles underneath my skin and in my scalp and to run electricity through my body just to develop the research on these cells.*

> *It's not the cure.*

It's a lot of work. You have to be mentally prepared for that. And the biggest thing is that I have the right at any time to just stop showing up. To refuse to keep on going. At any time, I can just say I don't feel like traveling to Switzerland. It's too long of a trip. Sorry. And they'd just have to say, "Okay." That really hurts the research. And that's what's happened with a few people in these studies, where they've dropped out because of lifestyle changes back home, they don't want to do long trips anymore, they're tired of the examinations, they get frustrated and upset about them — it's all too painful, long, and exhausting.

The people who raise their hands and volunteer to be first can hardly be thanked enough. They're not necessarily going to get anything back, especially in a safety study where the number of cells going into their spinal cords is so tiny. They might end up with more pain, or even less function than they had before. Without these people, though, no one will ever be able to make a case for trying a real dose, much less make it available to everyone who needs it.

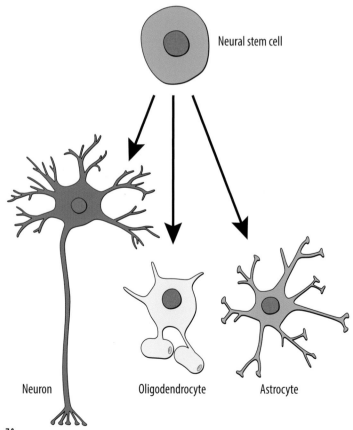

Neural stem cell

Neuron

Oligodendrocyte

Astrocyte

Neural stem cells. It seems so logical, right? But these are still visitors from another galaxy, from another human being. It's true that doctors have been doing transplants from one human to another for a long, long time — but those transplants are either organs (like kidneys, lungs, heart) or tissues (like skin, veins, tendons). Cells are different. They could grow out of control and form tumors. They could migrate to places where they don't belong. Organs and tissues never do that.

So far, though, all is well. Both StemCells, Inc. and the other company currently doing neural stem cell transplants in people (Neuralstem, Inc.) are going strong. They're both recruiting paralyzed volunteers like Lee to help them move forward, and they're both publishing results that — so far — show no harm and point toward small, measurable changes in function. Neural stem cells might just be the best shot at a real cure, though it's definitely in the future. How *far* in the future is partially up to us.

11 No Fairy Dust, Please

The most wrenching dreams I have are the ones where I dream that this injury was itself a dream. It never happened to my family at all. It was just a really intense and vivid nightmare, and I will get to wake up in a world where everything is normal.

In these dreams March 7, 2001, was just another Wednesday in early spring. Nobody went skiing that day, and we all slept through that night in our own beds, just like always. March 8th was a regular Thursday. I taught my classes and focused on writing the novel I'd been researching. Bruce went to work and the girls went to school.

What actually happened is that my husband spent that night in the ER and later in the Neuro Intensive Care Unit, I spent it in terror with friends in a series of waiting rooms, and the girls spent it at our house with a kind stranger, separated from us both. Nobody went to work for a very long time, and today I'm writing about advocacy and science instead of fictional people.

When I wake up from these dreams, there's always a split second when I think, "Wow," and then glance across the room. *Right. Wheelchair parked next to our bed.* It wasn't a bad dream. It all happened for real. At that moment, what I want most is magic; I want some fairy dust that could be sprinkled over my husband and make this all go away.

But there's no way to unturn a calendar page or reverse a clock. When we talk about doing our part to find faster cures for spinal cord injury, we can't be talking about magic… what we choose to fight for has to be as solid as the keyboard under my fingers right now. I bring this up because in some parts of our community there's a belief that if we could only invest enough money into one particular area, cures would be found, and quickly.

It's time to talk about human embryonic stem cells.

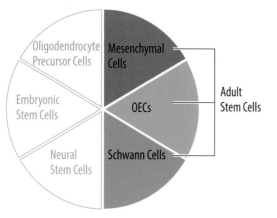

Don't get me wrong; I see the potential in these cells and I fully support the many investigations going on around the world that will one day lead to therapies for suffering people. My issue is with the word, *quickly*. What I want to be clear about is that human embryonic stem cells are not magic, at least not in the sense that they're a simple, easy solution for us.

We've been talking for the last couple of chapters about the possibility of finding a way to replace the three kinds of cells in the spinal cord that were lost or damaged by the injury. Some of these potential replacement cells exist in our own bodies; they're often called "adult" stem cells even though infants have them, too. They're on the right side of the circle. We know that these cells can't really replace what's been lost, but scientists have been looking hard for ways to use them to help repair damage anyway.

The word embryo literally means **swelling within.** Ironically, by the time the swelling is visible (at around three months), the embryo has become a fetus.

Other kinds of cells only exist during *gestation* — the nine months between the moment of conception and the moment of birth. Conception — formally, the creation of a *zygote* — is an event during which a cell from one human exchanges and mixes its DNA with the DNA of another human. The word, *zygote*, reflects the extraordinary nature of that event. It comes from a word that means yoked; a zygote is the yoked-together genes of two people, mixed and combined to form a third.

Gestation is commonly sorted in terms of the stages of development, all the way from the joining of egg and sperm to an actual living, breathing, crying infant. *Fetus* is the name we give to the newly forming human being during the last seven months of pregnancy; before the fetus comes the *embryo*. The embryo stage is quite short, beginning at around three weeks post conception and lasting about five weeks.

When we're talking about *human embryonic stem cells,* we're actually referring to cells that exist in the stage even before the embryo — a brief period of nine or ten days during which the original single-celled zygote is busy building perfect replicas of itself to form a tiny ball, about the size of the period at the end of this sentence. The innermost layer of that ball is what will become the embryo. During that pre-embryo stage of growth, this early version of what could be transformed into a living, breathing, thinking human person is known as a *blastocyst*. *Blasto* means *germ* or *seed*; this ball is the seed of a person.

The blastocyst, finally, gets us to the conversation about human embryonic stem cells, because that's what blastocysts are made of. That inner sphere is a bundle of identical cells. It has a very, very short lifespan — just a little more than a week passes while all the cells in that ball are exactly the same. Once that period is over, the cells begin to differentiate, and the blastocyst becomes an embryo.

The argument for using these undifferentiated blastocyst cells to treat spinal cord injury goes like this:

- Cells inside a blastocyst can obviously become the kinds of cells we need to replace in our damaged cords. They can turn into neurons, astrocytes, and oligodendrocytes. We know this for sure, because they're what became those kinds of cells.
- There is a large source of healthy blastocysts that — if not used for research and eventual cures — will become medical waste. The procedure known as in-vitro fertilization nearly always results in the formation of more blastocysts than a couple looking to make a family will ever want or be able to raise. There are hundreds of thousands of blastocysts frozen in fertility clinics all over the world. As many as one-fifth of the potential parents have told researchers that they intend to pay for their storage indefinitely. Many others pay for storage for a time and then quietly consign the excess blastocysts to the medical waste bin.
- If enough money and talent were invested in finding ways to make use of the cells inside those blastocysts, unfathomable needless suffering would end.

The argument against using them goes like this:

- Blastocysts aren't human "seeds." In a real sense, they're unique human beings with their own unique DNA. The fact that they are

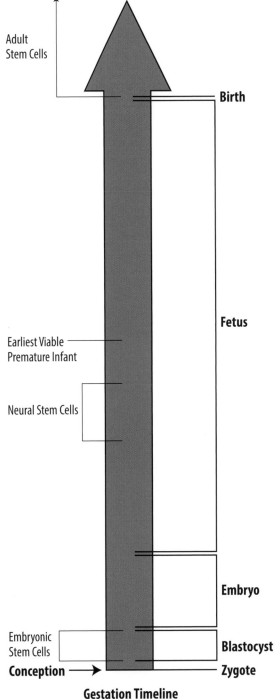

75

microscopically small and undeveloped does not change this fact.
- There is a permanent and clear moral prohibition against sacrificing one person for the benefit of another. Every person is equally precious. Because each blastocyst is a unique and precious human being, there can be no scenario in which any of them should be sacrificed, no matter how compelling the need.
- In the long run, it's more just and humane to find other, less troubling ways to end suffering.

Here's what I think. On the day we as a culture decided that it was okay to help infertile couples use the in-vitro procedures, we also decided that it was okay to create these hundreds of thousands of "surplus" blastocysts. We did not, however, have a discussion up front about what that would mean. We seem to be content to let this strange situation continue, at least for the time being.

I know a couple of young men who were born as a result of an in-vitro procedure. They're a joy to everyone who knows them — athletic, ambitious, kind, and very funny guys. Without the procedure, they wouldn't exist. Their parents, who are old friends of ours, decided long ago to donate several surplus blastocysts to science, which is within their rights by our laws. I know another couple with a pair of brilliant adult daughters who faced the same choice. They were unable to do it... those blastocysts could have become more children, and it just seemed wrong. They had, after all, seen the images of the blastocysts that eventually became their girls.

On the other hand, they were paying a steep storage fee every month, which made no sense given that they knew they'd never be able to support more children. They made the decision to thaw the blastocysts (which of course would end their existence) and then figure out how to create some kind of private ritual to mark the event and honor these lost potential lives. The clinic told them to forget it. Medical waste. Has to be disposed of according to regulations. Sorry.

I tell these stories to underline the weird and contradictory approach we've collectively taken when it comes to our thinking on the most readily available source of human embryonic stem cells. We don't seem to know what we think or why we think it, and the result has been a muddle. Any advocate who wants to press for more funding and resources to be devoted to this arm of research has to be prepared to confront that muddle.

But what about the science itself? Isn't it the case that these cells really could be the answer to the question of how to get replacements for our lost neurons? The answer to that question is a big, loud *maybe*. These cells are not fairy dust. They're living things with very definite agendas of their own. Remember that the blastocyst stage only lasts a bit more than a week, and that what happens next is the cells start differentiating. They start to transform themselves into other kinds of cells according to a strict and complex set of biological rules. It's not at all obvious how to manage that process in a dish, and it's even less obvious how to manage it inside the body of an adult with a damaged spinal cord.

I'm saying, there's no reason to think that transplanting these purest of cells into your body or mine would have any particular result. Maybe they'd die off. Maybe they'd continue to reproduce copies of themselves and form tumors. Maybe they'd differentiate into cell types that aren't helpful. When scientists talk about needing to do more basic science before trying to use these cells on people, this is the kind of question they're trying to answer: *What exactly makes an embryonic stem cell decide to become a neuron, anyway?* Knowing just that much is massively challenging.

And yet there are places where doctors are claiming to cure patients by injecting embryonic stem cells into their bodies. One of them is Dr. Geeta Shroff's small clinic in New Delhi, India. Dr. Shroff is an in-vitro fertilization specialist who claims to have used a single donated blastocyst from one of her patients to create a pure population of embryonic stem cells. She says that this cell population has been thriving at her clinic since 2002, and one Indian newspaper reports that as of 2012 her team had injected these cells into more than a thousand patients, at least a hundred of whom came from the USA.

One of those patients is the son of my friend, Matt Rodreick. Matt is, I suspect, a lot like many of you who are choosing to read a book like this one. He wants to understand things for himself. He's wired to question authority. He feels capable of assessing risk and benefit, and he knows that there really is a giant structural barrier when it comes to speed in medical innovation.

When I talked with Matt about the decision he made to take his son to India in the hope of some recovery, he described a process of reaching out to people who had themselves gone to Dr. Shroff's clinic. He met with at least one of them in person

It costs about $25,000 for each treatment in New Delhi, but the clinic offers it at no cost to about 15% of those who apply. The arithmetic says that the clinic must therefore have earned more than $20 million between 2002 and 2012.

and talked with others on the phone or online. He considered other options, including going to Portugal for the Dr. Lima procedure, going to China or Brazil, or of course simply waiting for something to become available here in the USA. He says that the deciding factor was about Dr. Shroff's "organic" approach:

> The thing that always brought me back to Geeta was the fact that people were doing physical therapy. And for whatever reason, as I look back I think there were the beginnings of activity-based therapy and writing about this new sort of rehab modality. It must have been that I started to link the two. That you can't just go to China for a week and have a surgery and go home. There was this notion that you have to be actually placing demand on the body at the same time that you're getting some treatment. And it felt like Geeta's model was different than everybody else's out there. It was this long stay, and it was coupled with twice a day PT, and once on Saturdays. And there were multiple interventions — not just one surgical procedure, but ten or eleven or twelve even, over the course of three months.

And so Matt and his son went to live New Delhi for a season. Since that time, Matt has become a respected and well-informed advocate for more funding for research. The same willingness to question authority, stick with a plan, take risks, and refuse to give up is now aimed at the establishment here, because it seems like a better bet in the long run. Asked if he'd do the India trip again, knowing what he knows today, Matt said probably not.

> I still have the same sort of assessment of Geeta. I'm not convinced that what she has is "the shit" — but I'm also not convinced that she's a charlatan. What I do think is — let's say she's not a charlatan, and she's actually got something. What I know from my conversations with her and with her anesthesiologist, whom I also talked with extensively, is that even if she has some wonderful line of cells, what I'm convinced of is that she doesn't know exactly what to do with them. And that she's really kind of throwing them at the wall to find something that will stick.

This is the issue, of course, with therapies that haven't been rigorously tested. They might work for some people, or they might work for some conditions, or they might work at certain time points — but it's impossible to know what the rules are that determine the outcomes. We need to know the rules by which embryonic stem cells operate before it makes sense to try them in people.

They're not fairy dust.

When I think of the way Dr. Shroff and others have been injecting these cells into patients, the image that comes to mind is a giant sculpture made of blown glass, like the ones that are displayed in buildings all over Seattle. It's like the damaged spinal cord is one of these — a fantastically elaborate structure, unbelievably fragile and shimmering with color and light. It has a tiny crack, though, hidden deep in the twists and folds of glass. Because the original structure was formed from pure silica sand, the idea that repair might involve silica sand makes sense.

But you wouldn't just toss a handful of sand onto the glass and hope that it would find its way to the crack. A sculpture made of blown glass, like a human spinal cord, is the result of an orderly, well-defined process. Repairing it will need to be at least as orderly and just as well-defined.

12 Placing the Very First Bet

We're at the last section of the circle when it comes to replacing lost cells. This section has to do with a project we talked about way back in Chapter 2: the cells known as oligodendrocyte precursors. Here's a quick review.

Oligodendrocytes are those crazy-looking octopus cells — the ones with lots of arms that reach out and wrap blobs of myelin around nearby axons. The axons need the myelin blobs in order to send signals. *No myelin* doesn't mean *no signal*; it just means a really, really slow and possibly distorted signal. When a spinal cord is damaged, one of the things that happens is that those wrapper cells get killed. Sometimes the axons themselves are still okay and even still connected, but they don't work well because they've lost too much myelin, and there aren't any oligodendrocytes to replace it.

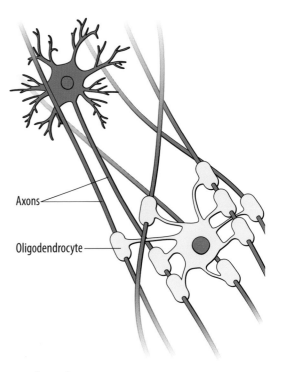

Axons

Oligodendrocyte

What's interesting is that there are some cells in a normal, healthy spinal cord called *oligodendrocyte precursors*. I described these as "vice-presidents," because they can only become one thing and only under one specific circumstance. They can become wrapper cells when existing oligodendrocytes are damaged. The problem is that there aren't enough of these vice-presidents to replace all the wrapper cells that get destroyed in an injury situation. But — and this is the important part — the spinal cord is friendly to them. It's their natural habitat, in a sense.

These cells could fit right in at the party. They know the language, they're wearing the right clothes, they're able to eat the food, and they even recognize friends in the room. The question is, *if there aren't enough in your own body to replace all the ones that were lost, where would you get some more?*

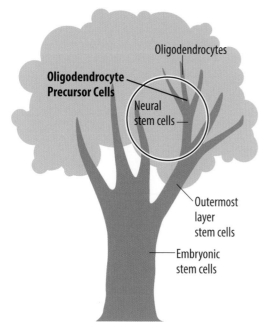

Oligodendrocytes

Oligodendrocyte Precursor Cells

Neural stem cells

Outermost layer stem cells

Embryonic stem cells

Back to the tree. One option would be to figure out the exact place in fetal development where one of the neural stem cells differentiates to become a wrapper cell precursor, then find a way to harvest those cells, purify them, keep them alive, and see what would happen if they could be transplanted into a damaged cord.

Another option would be to begin with a healthy and pure embryonic stem cell, then figure out how to get it to take that same development path in a dish instead of within a developing embryo. If that could be done, there would be a ready supply of these critters. Problem solved.

It seems like such a long, long shot. There are so many ways and times this approach could fail, beginning with the reality that it's very difficult to reproduce even this single development trail in a lab dish and ending with the question of how much good a little more myelin could really do. We don't even know for sure how many axons survive after an injury, much less which ones or what function might be restored to us if those axons got their myelin back.

And yet, it happened. Scientists working at the Reeve-Irvine Research Center managed to take an embryonic stem cell in a dish and get it to differentiate exactly as it would in a developing human. They grew pure populations of those wrapper cell precursors — millions of little vice-presidents all set to become oligodendrocytes when placed into what would be for them a friendly and welcoming environment: a damaged spinal cord. If you're like me, at this point you might be wondering how on earth that's possible — or even how it works that a ball of identical cells differentiates at all. What makes one cell turn into part of the heart muscle and another become the structure of a bit of skin? If the cells are all exactly alike, how can they know how to do different things? How do they become different from one another?

We don't really need the formal textbook explanation for how that works, but it helps me to at least have a good metaphor. Think of that ball of identical cells as a group of blind musicians, each one capable of playing every instrument in an orchestra. They are novice players with unlimited potential, standing in a huddle, surrounded by four open doors. At this point, each one has the very same instruction, which is to move through a door. If they don't move, they die.

That's the situation with all the stem cells in a blastocyst. They must begin to differentiate within a few days of conception; no pure stem cells can remain. And so the plain players drift at random through the doors. Each door represents a different section of the orchestra: woodwinds, brass, strings, percussion. As a player passes through a door, his ability to play the instruments outside his section is lost. When embryonic stem cells pass through one of the four doors available to them at the first branching of the tree, their ability to function along another branch is lost.

Once inside a door, each musician begins to sound the notes that can be made within his section. Once a cell has taken a particular path, it does a similar thing, sending out chemical signals to nearby cells. Those signals are made of proteins — molecules manufactured by the cells themselves according to recipes written into the cell's DNA. A cell can no more send a "wrong" signal than a man with a violin could play notes on the bass clef.

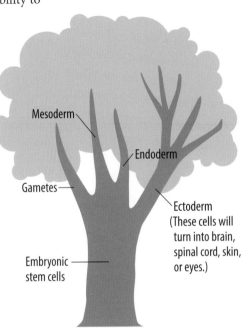

The blind musicians are traveling toward the orchestra pit, listening and adjusting their tone and timing so that the sounds they make fit into the music they hear. This is how they tune their instruments and learn their parts. Likewise, cells can communicate with each other by way of molecules, which is how they know which particular paths to take and which to avoid. In the end, once all the differentiating is complete, there will be 200 different types of cells in the finished body. And some of them will be oligodendrocyte precursors.

What the Irvine scientists did, then, was to figure out exactly what protein cues are naturally given to a cell once it begins to drift into the branch of the tree whose tips contain wrapper cells. Those molecules, properly timed and produced in the correct order and dose, are how the cells get their instructions. The whole process is known as *pre-differentiation*.

It's the exact opposite of tossing embryonic stem cells into a grown body and expecting them to automatically know what to do — instead, pre-differentiation takes those same embryonic stem cells and gets them ready to fit into an existing system. The plan with these vice-presidents was that they would be in an environment where every local protein signal would be saying, *Finish the job. Become a wrapper cell. Produce myelin. Wrap myelin on those axons right over there.*

Hey, it worked in rats.

Well, sort of. The way you measure how well a treatment works in rat studies is with what's called the *BBB Scale*. The scale goes from zero to twenty-one. Rats with new injuries are at zero, where they all stay for the first three or four days. Then during the next week or so, most of them get back to about an eleven on the scale all on their own. Eleven means they can move and maybe take steps, but they're uncoordinated and their walking isn't really functional. For untreated rats, that's as good as it gets.

The rats in the wrapper cell study got to about thirteen on the scale during the first couple of weeks, and then they kept improving for a few more days, climbing to an average score of about sixteen. After that they didn't get any better. A score of sixteen on a scale of zero to twenty-one isn't bad, right? But it's also not all *that* much better than a score of eleven. The treated rats could do some coordinated stepping using all four paws, and the untreated rats couldn't do any.

The scientist who gets credit for pulling this off is named Dr. Hans Keirstead. A big part of his success in finding funding for his lab has to do with how appealing and articulate he is. The guy was the subject of a spread in **Men's Vogue**. He was once named one of the hottest people in Orange County, California. He was a big hit on **60 Minutes** with his cage of walking rats. Good looks are an asset for scientists, just like everybody else.

Pre-Differentiation Research Timeline

1998 human embryonic stem cells first isolated, in work funded by a private company called Geron

2002 animal studies using pre-differentiated cells designed at UC Irvine

2005 publication of results from animal studies

2005 Dr. Keirstead forms private company, CA Stem Cells, Inc.

1995   2000   2005

That rat study from Dr. Hans Keirstead's lab is what eventually got those precursor cells tested in people. I've made a timeline to give you an idea of what a long haul it was for his team.

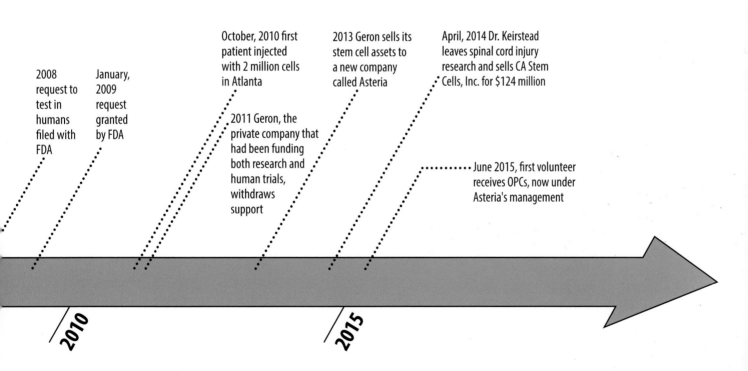

2008 request to test in humans filed with FDA

January, 2009 request granted by FDA

October, 2010 first patient injected with 2 million cells in Atlanta

2011 Geron, the private company that had been funding both research and human trials, withdraws support

2013 Geron sells its stem cell assets to a new company called Asteria

April, 2014 Dr. Keirstead leaves spinal cord injury research and sells CA Stem Cells, Inc. for $124 million

June 2015, first volunteer receives OPCs, now under Asteria's management

2010

2015

I think the most interesting thing about that timeline is the story it tells about money in the research world. Later we'll get into detail about how that works, but for now it's worth noting two things: One is that the move from animal studies to human trials was so expensive that Geron bailed on it after having spent about $20 million dollars and more than a dozen years trying to get there. The other is that it's possible to get rich doing research, even if you haven't cured anything yet.

So, where are we today with respect to the wrapper cell replacement strategy? Hard to say. We know that a small dose of the cells hasn't done any harm to the first five patients who were given them, at least not yet, and it's been more than four years since Patient #1 got the cells in Atlanta. So that's good. We don't know if a real dose might have helped him regain some function, because he didn't get a real dose — he got a tiny taste.

We know that the patients who get these cells during 2015 will be getting about 10 times as many cells as the first patients got, which may or may not tell us something about how effective those cells are. When scientists design these trials, they're doing some guessing; they have to, because there's no way of knowing how closely a person's body will mirror what happens in a rat.

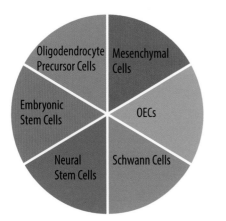

Before we leave the cell replacement section, let's have one more look at the big picture. Our circle has six sections, each one representing a type of cell and a strategy for recovery. Those on the right half are all cells found inside your own body right now, which means your immune system will leave them alone. One problem with them is that none of them can ever become one of the kinds of cells that were lost in the injury. Another problem is that if it does turn out that they're helpful in restoring function, we'll need an efficient and reliable way to collect and purify them for every possible patient.

On the left side are three types of cells that come from outside your body; these are cells either taken directly from a human blastocyst or from fetal material. These kinds of cells can be manufactured in large numbers and kept pure, just like any other kind of drug. A serious issue, though, is that anyone getting one of these cell types will have to have their immune responses temporarily suppressed in order for the cells to stay alive; this is a danger because we rely on our immune systems to protect us from all kinds of sickness and infection.

There's one type of cell I haven't included in the picture until now: it's called an iPSC, which stands for *induced pluripotent stem cell*. These are cells that behave like embryonic stem cells — but they're taken not from blastocysts but rather created from cells taken from adult bodies. That means, in a sense, that they're on both sides of the circle at once.

Wait, what? That's right. Sir John Gurdun and Shinya Yamanaka shared a Nobel Prize in medicine a few years ago for figuring out how to pull off that small miracle. They showed that it's possible to take a skin cell and wind its clock all the way back to the blastocyst stage. The best thing about being on the right side of the circle applies to iPSCs: they're made from your own cells, so your immune system will let them thrive. They also require no use of human blastocysts if that's something that troubles you. The worst thing about being on the right side of the circle applies, too, though. Right now there's no practical way to create them and ensure purity on a patient-by-patient basis.

Likewise, iPSCs have all the good and bad qualities of the cells on the left side of the circle: they can be made in as big a batch as needed and kept for a reasonable time period. They can potentially be nursed along whatever development path you like to become whatever kind of cell you need. And they can get out of control and form tumors.

You'll have realized by now that getting *any* cell replacement therapies on the market is going to be difficult, complicated, and expensive. That's true for "adult" cells, it's true for "embryonic" cells, and it's true for induced pluripotent stem cells. We aren't going to see these cells for sale anytime soon.

I don't think that's a reason to give up.

I think we're like the pioneers who opened up the American West. They slogged their way across the plains at great expense and trouble. When they arrived, they had to build hasty shelters and figure out how they were going to stay fed. Eventually it became possible to create the roads and structures that make life livable.

For us, demanding research into cell replacement science is like making that sort of long-term investment. We do it because we'll learn things as we go, and because the others that follow are depending on us. Thousands and thousands of people are going to become paralyzed this year, and next year, and the year after that.

We want the permanent structures to be there for those people. In the meantime, for the first time, we can look at some treatments that could be available for *us* in the near term. The very near term.

Part Three

Getting Lucky

13 The Long Slog

In 1968 I was a teenager living in northwestern lower Michigan, blissfully indifferent to things like paralysis and bowel programs. The Beatles were still together and still putting out new albums. A gallon of gas went for 34 cents, and you could buy a house for under $15,000. The minimum wage was $1.60. Two of my older brothers were in Vietnam. I had an after-school job at a local drugstore, where I cooked terrible, greasy food from behind a long green counter and served it to people who couldn't afford to eat at a real restaurant.

It was, in other words, a really long time ago.

Just a few hours south of me was Michigan State University, where a young scientist named Reggie Edgerton was finishing up his PhD in Exercise Physiology. Exercise Physiology is what people study when they want to become sports trainers or strength coaches. Exercise Physiologists work in health clubs. They supervise programs for fitness. And some of them do research, trying to understand how exercise changes the way the human body functions.

Luckily for us, Reggie was one of those. He took that PhD and went off to get to work in southern California, where he's been teaching and studying exercise ever since. I bring all this up not because the history matters to you or me, but because it's important to recognize that this section of the book is a classic example of the philosopher Seneca's definition of luck:

It's what happens when preparation meets opportunity.

Reggie and many of the people he's mentored over the last 40 years hit a sort of jackpot recently, and that jackpot is the subject of these next few chapters. These scientists got lucky, meaning that their long, intense preparation intersected in a totally surprising way with a particular set of circumstances.

I said back in Chapter 4 that the spinal cord has turned out to be smart — capable of learning new things and remembering them, but only under the right circumstances and with the right kinds of teachers. Do we have those factors nailed down yet? We don't… but we're a lot closer than we used to be. Not too long after my husband's injury, someone sent us a little booklet about a guy from Minnesota who had been injured for about 30 years. The booklet was a heartfelt tribute to this man's life — his energy, humor, determination, and courage.

I remember reading about how he'd built himself a home gym, including a full set of parallel bars that stood in his living room for the first 10 years after he got hurt. He was convinced that if he just worked hard enough and long enough, he could get his dead lower body working again. And so he would haul himself along those bars every day of every week, willing his feet to take steps. They never did. He only gave up when it became clear that he was doing serious damage to his shoulders in the effort.

He was up against a problem he had no way to recognize: the part of his cord that was down below his injury and still perfectly okay couldn't be re-trained without two things: help and very specific input. The very specific input he needed had to take the form of his own feet and legs telling his spinal cord that they were moving and bearing weight. For a guy like him, that meant what's known as *body-weight-supported ambulation*. Simply, he needed something to hold him up, and something else to make his feet and legs move in a normal walking pattern. How do I know this? Because it's the one no-surgery-required thing that has actually helped some injured people to take steps — even a few with chronic injuries.

Body-weight-supported training is also called *locomotor* training. It's been tried with rats, cats, and monkeys in countries all over the world since the 1970s. And it's being done with people right now.

There was a preschooler named Kyle Bartolini, for example, who got shot in a drive-by at the age of three. His parents had been told that Kyle would never sit up or use his hands again, much less be able to stand or walk. He couldn't stand unassisted or move his legs at all, and that was not supposed to change. About a year and a half after his injury, they volunteered him for a study. That boy got seventy-six training sessions, each one requiring a harness and three people to keep him stabilized over a moving treadmill while his feet were placed by hand on the belt as it rolled slowly beneath him.

After about a month of those sessions, the kid began to take steps on his own; by the end of the study he was getting around fine behind a walker. It's a frustrating thing to read about, in some ways. It works, but definitely not for everybody. And even if it did always work, it's not scalable. There's just no way that every person sitting in a wheelchair right now is going to have seventy-six sessions of personalized training, or even one session. There's also no way to know which people would benefit and which ones would leave frustrated and (presumably) a lot poorer.

In that sense, locomotor training is a lot like the Panama City give-me-some-stem-cells kind of plan, though without the plane tickets and with a lot less risk. It may or may not change anything. Only the very well-off can afford it. There's another option, though, besides paying three experienced trainers to place your feet for you: a piece of equipment called a Lokomat that costs about $300,000. The drawback there is that you have to live near one in order to pay the hourly rate to use it, and that leaves out everybody who happens to live in about 20 states. So, if our determined friend from Minnesota had been able to sign up for that sort of program, would it have helped him?

Maybe. The likelihood is that he'd have needed some input, too. That's where the lucky break enters the story. Before we get to talking about that, though, we need to set the stage a little by mentioning something everybody hates: neuropathic pain.

It's the worst.

Our friends who live in not-paralyzed-land are usually surprised to hear that it hurts to have a spinal cord injury. I think they imagine that it's as if your whole lower body just goes *poof* — no pain, no pleasure, no feeling. When we tell them the actual story, they get a cringey look on their faces. Neuropathic pain is no joke. I read one study that said four out of five people with spinal cord injuries suffer from it, and most of them get only partial, temporary relief from drugs and other strategies.

Here's a handy chart with some very rough information about that; it's taken from a survey done in 2006. It shows what a hopeless situation this can be for the 80% of us who live with neuropathic pain, especially for the people who have it bad.

Every so often I wake up to find my husband lying next to me with all the covers off him, silently waiting for the neuropathic pain attack to subside. He can't stand to have even a sheet touching him at those times, and he hasn't found a better way to deal with it than just to suffer and wait until it's over.

Drug or method	Percentage who have ever tried it / percentage who are using it now (rounded to nearest whole)	How much relief on a scale of 0-10, where 0 = none, 10 = total bliss?
Gabapentin (aka neurontin)	38 / 17	3.3
Anti-depressants	41 / 10	2.9
Medical marijuana	32 / 20	6.6
Acupuncture	28 / 3	3.5
Hypnosis	9 / 3	2.9
Valium	39 / 18	4.5

The middle column is sort of a reflection of the last one, right? Something that works better is probably going to have more people sticking with it, assuming the side effects aren't too horrible and you can afford it. What I really found surprising, though, is how many people just deal with low-to-medium level neuropathic pain by ignoring it. Also, notice that medical pot — according to the people who answered this survey — works *twice* as well as gabapentin in terms of relief. It's still illegal in more than half the states, though, so there's that issue. Having neuropathic pain in jail is really not something anybody would want to try.

It would be great if there were some kind of device that could interrupt pain — some small gizmo that could trick the nervous system into not sending those signals. So far, there's no such thing for us, but some companies — including one called *Medtronic* — have been selling what's known as a *spine implant* for years.

A spine implant is really four things:

- A little remote control that you can hold in your hand
- A pulse generator that's sewn into a pocket under your skin
- An extension wire
- An array of electrodes with leads going to the wire

For about half the people with chronic back pain *not* related to spinal cord injury, the spine implant works pretty well. It's been tested on us, too, but alas. It doesn't help with neuropathic pain. Scientists aren't exactly sure what makes it stop regular back pain; the theory is that the low-level electrical charge changes the way the brain interprets pain signals coming up through the cord.

So if the thing doesn't help us with neuropathic pain, why should we care? *Because it's already on the market, and because when it was tested in people living with paralysis, it didn't cause any damage.* We can use it for other purposes, off the shelf.

It was natural that when Dr. Reggie Edgerton and others were looking for an implant that might provide some help to a person's spinal cord, they decided to try that one. Remember that even the best body-weight-supported training almost never works for people with zero motor function. Even if our guy from Minnesota had been able to get himself suspended over a treadmill with skilled assistants moving his feet, he probably wouldn't have regained any ability to move on his own.

He needed a boost. It's funny, but cats with completely broken spinal cords can be trained to walk and stand just through body-weight-supported training. Rats, on the other hand, can only get there if they're *also* given a little bit of electrical stimulation. And it turns out that in this instance, people are more like rats than cats. I'm not talking about giving an electrical jolt to a particular muscle or muscle group, but instead about sending a very low-level impulse into the part of an intact cord that's way below the injury, down near the tailbone.

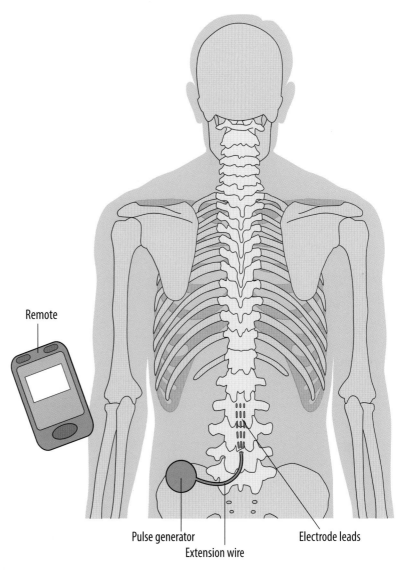

Remote

Pulse generator

Extension wire

Electrode leads

The first person to get one of those Medtronic gizmos was named Rob Summers. You can think of Rob as a young, west-coast version of that optimistic Minnesotan, unable to take no for an answer no matter how often he heard it or from how many experts. Rob was a college baseball star looking to get into the major leagues on the morning that he went out to get his gym bag out of his parked car and got knocked to the ground by a hit-and-run driver.

His injury was at T1; not one of his muscles below that level had fired in more than a year when he was first suspended over a treadmill in Louisville, KY in October of 2007. He spent the next two years getting intensive body-weight-supported training from one of the most capable teams in the world, and nothing happened. In November of 2009, after 170 training sessions, the tests showed exactly what they'd showed on the day he arrived.

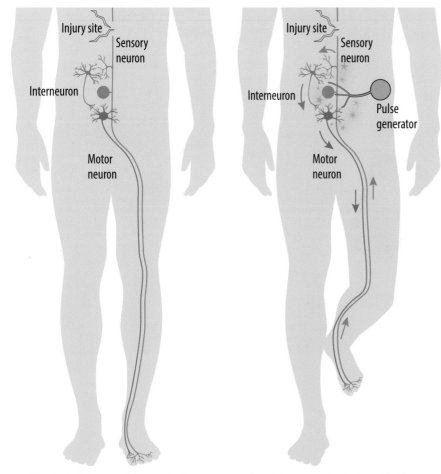

The circuits below your injury are in place, but they don't do anything useful

Same injury, same circuits, but with faint electrical pulses delivered. Now the circuits are awake, and the feet/knees/ankles can move

Not a single muscle firing, not even a trace of a wisp of a signal.

And then just before Christmas of 2009, he signed the consent forms and they put the spinal cord stimulator into his lower back. After giving him a couple of weeks to recover from the surgery, they got him back up over the treadmill. What happened then was great, but it wasn't really a surprise to the researchers. With the stimulator turned on and giving a boost to the neural networks in his lower cord, Rob learned to bear his own weight. The muscles in his trunk, hips, legs, and feet started firing. He was very far from being able to step off the treadmill, but the testing equipment showed that with the stimulator turned on, he wasn't "motor complete" anymore.

This was similar to how it had worked in multiple rat studies. Reggie Edgerton has described the low-level stimulation as like changing the "mood" of the lower cord, so that when Rob was placed on his feet, the networks of linked interneurons and motor neurons and sensory neurons kicked in, and his muscles responded. Rob himself told me that it's like turning up the volume of a station you can't quite hear.

That was exciting enough, but what happened next was a game-changer. It was luck in the exact sense that Seneca defined it: a moment when preparation and opportunity shook hands. The long slog that so many scientists had been on since the '60s had led them into new, undreamt-of territory.

14 Surprised in a Good Way

We were screwing around in the lab one day, about seven months after I'd gotten the stimulator. I was lying down on the mat, and somebody said, more or less as a joke, "Hey, Rob, move your foot." And I did.

That was the surprise. Up until that moment, the team of scientists working with Rob had been pretty sure they understood how the stimulator combined with careful step and stand training to get the muscles in his lower body working. They were using the implant to boost the general level of excitement in the lower spinal cord while simultaneously using their suspended-body-weight training to push sensory information into his system from outside.

Excite the neural networks in the presence of artificial standing and stepping: that was the agenda. Turn up the inner volume. Stand him up and move him so his feet, ankles, knees, and hips would be bombarded with the old familiar sensations.

But when Rob was just lying down on an exercise mat there were no helpful sensory cues coming in. No changing pressure on the bottoms of his feet. No clues from posture that he was in mid-stride. Nothing. The stimulator was on, but by itself that shouldn't have been enough, any more than all those 170 training sessions he'd had before he got it implanted were enough. The thinking was, you needed both.

Rob's role in this case study was supposed to be Human Guinea Pig. He was a young guy with a complete injury who volunteered to let himself be used in order to help the scientists understand more about where

What we did with the implant was to first map the circuitry there. We did many experiments to understand what the physiology of that circuitry was. And then we started combining it with the sensory cues… the sensory information is what's really the driver for the final pattern.

So we had to balance and find which stimulation parameters would put the circuitry in the most appropriate state for standing or for walking. And then we continued on, and we did training sessions, an hour a day.

Dr. Susan Harkema, June, 2011

and how to place those electrodes and how much electricity to shoot through them. That was the goal. Everybody knew that the Medtronic pain device wasn't going to be the final product if there ever was one. It was just a convenient place to start. Rob wasn't supposed to get anything out of this study except the satisfaction of moving the science forward, plus hanging out with some really great people. Even if it all worked exactly as expected, he personally would not gain much. He wouldn't get better.

So when he moved his foot all by himself just because he wanted to, it meant that the scientists knew a lot less than they thought they had. Dr. Reggie Edgerton said, *"None of us believed that! I was afraid to believe it when we first saw it. But it's true."* Dr. Susan Harkema, a former student of Reggie's who was in charge of the Louisville team working with Rob, stopped everything when she realized what had happened. Rob describes her telling the team that they were going to have to start again and re-think the whole project.

It wasn't the cure. It wasn't the cure, but it was an opening into new territory, like the discovery of a hidden pass through forbidding mountains. With the stimulator sparking his lower cord neural networks, it turned out that Rob could move his toes, his ankles, and his legs without any sensory cues at all. With the stimulator off, he had no access to those muscle groups.

So, what was going on? Maybe a tiny group of axons had survived and were always there — coming down from brain neurons, but not in enough numbers to create the general level of excitement needed to kick the lower cord neural networks into gear. Maybe all that step and stand training had combined with the stimulation to somehow wake up broken axons and get them growing across the injury site. The one thing that couldn't be denied was that brain neurons were once again talking to neurons in the lower cord, at least with the juice turned on.

But there was more.

People who don't live with paralysis probably won't care so much about this one, but I do: after he'd had the implant for many months Rob could suddenly sweat. Yes! Nasty, smelly, plain old perspiration came back to him. He talks about the day he realized this while coaching a baseball game from his wheelchair. He was in Florida. It was a warm, humid day. He realized that his shirt was wet, and had that what-the-hell moment — and then it dawned on him that he'd been out in the sun for hours without even a hint of AD. His shirt was drenched with perspiration. He pulled out his phone, called Dr. Susan Harkema back in Louisville, and gave her the good news: *"Hi! Guess what? I'm sweating like a pig!"*

Now, how could that possibly be related to the low dose of electricity delivered to his cord? The stimulator wasn't even on when this happened. It also wasn't on when he realized that another lost experience had been restored: his orgasm was back. You won't be surprised to hear that this is the one thing almost everybody asks me about Rob Summers. *Can he…?* Yes. The answer is yes. In his words, *occasionally* — but until he got the stimulator it was *never*.

Well, okay. Here's the recap.

- College baseball star with a motor complete injury
- Three years go by with no return
- Two years of gait training, no return
- Stimulator implanted
- Seven months of gait training, increasing ability to stand and step with stimulator turned on and helpful sensory input provided
- Unexpected return of some muscles groups with stimulator on and no sensory input
- Unexpected return of some autonomic functions with no stimulation at all

To me, more than anything, Rob Summers represents about a thousand new questions. The first one is obvious.

Was it just him? Was there something special about his particular injury that made all this possible, or would the stimulator have a similar effect if it was implanted in other people? Dr. Susan Harkema wanted to know that, too. She recruited three more patients, but this time the protocol was different. Rob had been motor complete but not sensory complete; he'd been able to feel pinpricks and light touches in some areas of his lower body when he first arrived in Louisville.

> AD is **autonomic dysreflexia**. For those who need a reminder, it's that life-threatening thing you get when something is wrong in your body but your automatic systems don't correct it like they used to. When you're hot, you're supposed to sweat. If you have a spinal cord injury, you don't. Not sweating while your core temperature rises and rises is serious business. Untreated, it's a sure trip to the ER. It can kill you.

ASIA stands for **American Spinal Injury Association**. It's the group that came up with a rough classification system for the severity of injuries. The four levels (A, B, C, and D) go from most terrible to least terrible, in terms of movement and sensation.

The hypothesis was that maybe there was a connection between intact sensory neurons and the way that stimulator had kicked in. Maybe those surviving pathways going from Rob's skin all the way through his cord and up into his brain were the reason for the changes. It seemed like the most logical explanation, which is why two of the next three subjects in this experiment were guys with neither movement nor sensation. They were what we call ASIA A — the most devastating kind of injury. Can't move anything, can't feel anything, no signals getting through, period.

If having a few surviving sensory pathways was necessary, those guys would not get the kind of voluntary movement or autonomic system stuff that Rob did. That's what the Louisville team expected to see: a bunch of nothing. They also included a third person with an injury more like Rob's so they'd have a sense of whether this whole thing was just a fluke that would only work on Rob. Those four guys — the three new ones plus Rob — should give the scientists a feel for where the hidden mountain pass might lead. Two ASIA A, two ASIA B, all more than a couple of years post injury with no recovery.

The Louisville team started over with the body-weight-supported gait training. Before the new guys got their implants, all three of them were dangled over moving treadmills while scientists placed their feet in stepping movements. All three of them got at least 80 sessions like that, and nobody recovered any movement or even detectable signal to their muscles during that period. Then they got their implants and were allowed to rest for a few weeks. In Rob's case, almost a year of stand and step training happened after that rest period. Only then was he tested to see if he could move his feet without being in the harness, and he was only tested at all because someone made a joke one random day.

All of the new guys were tested for voluntary movement within days after the post-surgery rest period. And all of them could move their feet on command with the stimulator. *What?* It's true. Within days. No training. And they could move their feet, it turned out, with pretty good control. They could close their eyes and listen to a tone being changed in volume and match their movements to that volume. Louder, press harder. Softer, back off. They could watch a moving sine wave and time their movements to its rise and fall. This could only be instruction coming to the feet from the brain itself.

It wasn't the long months of post-implant step training that had fired up Rob's motor neurons. It wasn't the presence of his intact sensory pathways. It wasn't something unique about his particular body. The stimulator was responsible. A dumb little array of electrodes. Because I don't want any of you to imagine that the muscles themselves were somehow being tweaked, I'm going to remind us what the stimulator was not.

Most of us have at least heard of FES: *Functional Electrical Stimulation*. We have a little FES unit at our house, so I kind of know how it works. During the first season or two after my husband got sprung from the trauma center, we spent a part of each evening like this: he would lie on his stomach, and I would attach (with sticky tape) a set of flat square pads to pairs of specific spots on his just-barely-firing hamstrings. Wires came out of those pads and plugged into a black box with a dial to set the amount of current.

I'd turn on the juice and he would try as hard as he could to get his foot up off our mattress. Imagine a lot of grunting, as if he were bench-pressing 100 pounds. Usually he couldn't lift his foot at all, so I'd give him a head start and hold his ankle about half way to vertical. Then the current, the straining, and his foot would rise. That's FES, also known as "e-stim." It's a direct boost to a particular muscle, and for people like Bruce — who start out with a faint signal getting through — it can speed up strengthening. Lots of people use these things to make their legs move while sitting on a stationary bike, and they can build up muscles just as if the orders to push were coming from the brain instead of a box sitting next to the bike. Christopher Reeve was a big fan.

The stimulator that Dr. Susan Harkema's team of doctors implanted into the four young guys was a whole different animal. Instead of touching skin and aiming voltage at the muscle beneath that skin, it sat on top of the tough membrane that surrounds the whole spinal cord — the *dura*.

Outside the dura there's a gap created by the backside bones of your spine. It's called the *epidural space*, because the prefix *epi* means "on, upon, above." The epidural space is just the gap on top of the dura.

The stimulator goes into that epidural space, which is why this procedure is sometimes called epi-stim. Here's how one of the surgeons who put the device into Rob Summers described the whole rig:

15 A Better Mousetrap

The science of repairing spinal cord injury changed on the day that Rob Summers moved his foot on command. No cells had been replaced. There had been no removal of scar tissue from the injury site. No drugs, enzymes, or designer molecules had been added to his system. No genes had been altered. Logically, according to everything his doctors knew, what he was doing while lying on that mat should have been impossible.

But it clearly wasn't impossible.

Unfortunately, it's taking a while for the world to catch up with the news — and I'm talking about *us* as well as the general public and even the scientific community. It's one of those things that's so startling we think it must be a fluke. A mistake. Our "knowledge" about the damaged cord tells us that this can't happen.

What's going on is that our knowledge is really just a collection of assumptions. We're looking at evidence — Rob's moving foot — that says at least some of those assumptions have been wrong all along, but instead of asking what that means, a lot of people simply assume there's something wrong with the evidence.

This isn't the first time something like this has happened. During the late 1920s and early 1930s a German chemical company named Bayer made the exact same kind of error. Bayer was formed around the manufacture of beautiful dyes; its massive wealth grew from the creativity of its chemists, who were among the first to figure out how to make colors in a laboratory. The shades of red they could produce were astonishing, cheap to produce, and hugely popular. The dyes made them very rich.

So it's not surprising that they formed an almost religious devotion to the magic of those dyes. When they branched out into making drugs, many of their formulas began with dyes. In those days people routinely died from bacterial infections. Case of strep throat? You could be dead in a couple of weeks. Infected cut? Too bad. Nothing could be done. Every year women died by the tens of thousands from what was called "child-bed fever," ironically often spread by their doctors' failure to wash their hands between patients.

The Bayer company chemists were pretty excited, then, when they found that by adding a certain compound to one of their red dyes, they could easily cure these murderous infections within a few days. They thought that the compound — called *sulfanilamide* (sull-fa-NILL-uh-mide) — was a sort of key that unlocked the healing potential of their special red dye. They set about getting a patent for the combination and looked forward to even more wealth.

Unfortunately for them, it turned out that their dye wasn't what was making the patients better.

Sulfanilamide was the medicine. The dye was just coloring. Bayer's fancy patent was worthless, because sulfanilamide all by itself worked just fine — and it was available everywhere. French chemists figured this out within weeks of getting their hands on the Bayer product; it drove the Germans crazy.

Two things about this story remind me of the Rob Summers moment. One is that for the first two or three years, doctors all over Europe simply refused to believe the claims that were coming out of the Bayer labs. It was too good to be true. It didn't help that the Bayer managers weren't sharing their animal studies out of fear that someone would beat them to the market. But even after they published their data, interest remained low.

The other thing that reminds me of Rob's story is that one reason so many doctors dismissed the idea of Bayer's new drug was that it didn't fit what they thought they knew about how the body works. It didn't make sense to them that a drug could possibly kill off the bacteria so efficiently without harming the patient, too. The Bayer people, they thought, must be exaggerating.

What's happening now is a bit like that. In our community, I've heard all of the following:

- It's not really a cure, because they're only moving their feet a little.
- They can't pee normally, they just know when they have to go.
- They can't really empty their bladders.
- They're still not having sex like they used to.
- Who cares if they can stand up for a few minutes?
- I haven't seen anybody walk off a treadmill yet.
- It's not really a cure.

All of which is, I'm trying to say, beside the point. What we have in the epidural stimulator work isn't a cure for spinal cord injury — it's a revelation of faulty assumptions. And what we need next is to shake the cobwebs out and try to rearrange our thinking about the nature of a damaged cord. We need new experiments in epi-stim, and we need them done in such a way that we can depend on the results.

We don't want to be like those European doctors in 1934, shrugging off results that challenge what we think we already know. For example, we thought we knew that there was such a thing as a complete injury, in which axons coming down from neurons in the brain were either dead, not myelinated, or too few in number to make any useful connections. And yet there was Rob, with his motor complete injury. Clearly he had a population of living, myelinated axons getting through the injury site.

For another example, we thought we knew that the thinking part of the brain was so thoroughly in charge of our movement that it was running the whole show. That one seems odd though, right? It's obvious that almost all of what we do when we move around is done without conscious thought. It's automatic.

So, is this happening? Are we working out the kinks in the epi-stim technology? Not fast enough for my taste. There have been very promising experiments with various animals and epidural stimulators for *more than twenty years*, but until Rob no one had tried put one of these things into a human being with a spinal cord injury. Since Rob was implanted back at Christmas 2009, more than a dozen more paralyzed people have gotten implants. Only three of them are part of the published data.

Why would results not be published? There are only two reasons. One is that the experiments didn't show any change, and the other is that the papers are taking an extra long time to get through what is already a very slow process. I'm told by scientists researching this that the epidural results are good and showed change. So, the reason the results aren't published must be because of the publishing process. This is unacceptable.

We know that the stimulator Rob and the other three guys got in Louisville was an off-the-shelf model not even designed to do what it has done. What we need to know is, what does the next generation look like, and how do we get to it quickly?

To us, the Medtronic pain stimulator is like cars before the Model T. They weren't really much of an improvement over the old ways — but they pointed toward what might be possible. Those first cars were basically just horse buggies with engines. Drivers steered them like boats, with tillers. No headlights, turn signals, or mirrors. They could only be driven in the daylight, unless a friend walked a few steps ahead carrying a lantern to show the way.

Likewise, the pulse from the Medtronic device has to be adjusted by hand with the little remote. This isn't going to be the answer if we want more than body-weight-supported walking and being able to stand in a standing frame. And it's completely useless to people with no hand function. What we need — eventually — is a device that's responsive to our bodies in the same way that antilock brakes prevent our cars from skidding when we stomp on them hard. We need a device that reads the environment and adjusts automatically as that environment changes.

In addition to the scientists working with Dr Susan Harkema, there are others looking right now at the next generation device. One of them is at the University of California, Los Angeles, and another is in Lausanne, Switzerland, at the Swiss Federal Institute for Technology. The UCLA team is led by Dr. Reggie Edgerton, and his former student Dr. Gregoire Courtine is one of the people behind the work in Lausanne. The Lausanne researchers — according to their own reports — are focused on refining the implantable device. Okay, "refining" is not a strong enough word. They're starting from scratch and building the thing according to their own specifications. It does have the three basic parts I described earlier: an array of electrodes that lies along the dura just outside the cord, a small pulse generator that's embedded under the skin, and an outside control.

The Swiss version of an epidural stimulator is like a stretchy ribbon, designed to move and twist as if it were part of the dura itself

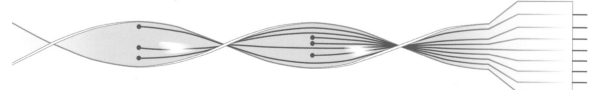

In the fall of 2014, their published work included this statement:

> *Animals with complete spinal cord injury performed more than 1000 successive*
> *steps without failure, and were able to climb staircases of various heights and*
> *lengths with precision and fluidity.*
>
> Science Translational Medicine, September, 2014

Precision and fluidity. I like the sound of that. They got these results by building a sophisti-cated feedback loop into their device's software. Unlike the Medtronic device, this one can tell which muscle groups are being engaged and at what strength and speed. Their device can adjust the pulse speed and placement as needed, all by itself.

Meanwhile at UCLA, Reggie's team has been working on its own impressive im-plantable device, but they've also got one that requires no surgery at all. It sits right on the skin of the lower back. They call the outside-the-body one a *transcutaneous* stimulator, which is just a lot of syllables to say that the pulse crosses the skin. (*Cutis* is the Latin word for skin.) They've also developed and tested a model that's getting results in upper body muscle groups: arms, hands, fingers.

This seems too good to be true. Just like the magic red elixir the Germans were claiming would cure every fatal case of strep throat, we have scientists saying that it's possible they've changed the rules about what it means (and doesn't mean) to have a spinal cord injury. I heard Reggie speak at a conference in late 2014, just weeks after the Lausanne group had published their paper about the precise and fluid movement of their transected rats.

The company working on these two spinal stimulators is called NeuroRecovery Technologies. They have patents pending for both devices, and in May of 2015 they began recruiting people to be part of a clinical trial with their transcutaneous stimulator. They're looking for functional return in both upper and lower extremities; if the devices work as well on us as they have on lab animals, it will be a different world.

The room was full of people in chairs. When he got to the part about his work with the transcutaneous stimulators, one guy asked what the work means for people like him, with incomplete injuries. This is what Reggie said:

> *People ask me why I wanted to start with completes, and I said offhandedly,*
> *"Because incompletes would be a piece of cake."*

A piece of cake. He gets to say that. He gets to say that after almost four decades of pa-tiently looking for the best way to understand what's going on in the bodies of people with damaged cords. He gets to say that after seeing his human subjects respond to the proto-types of the stimulators built in his lab. He gets to say that after seeing his students go out and move the technology along in parallel with his own team. It would be a piece of cake to get results for incompletes.

By now you'll have realized that I'm a fan of all this work with stimulators. I'm going to wrap up this section with some quick thoughts about how it has gotten this far and how we might help move it along. Ralph Waldo Emerson is supposed to have advised innovators this way, "Build a better mousetrap, and the world will beat a path to your door." He meant, of course, that improvement in a product will automatically translate into more sales.

But it isn't automatic. It can't happen at all if the product is poorly understood, if the im-provements are shrugged off, or most importantly, if the world doesn't know enough to care.

16 THE BIG IDEA

For the last year or so I've been watching the good people at the Christopher & Dana Reeve Foundation (CDRF) make a strong pitch to get 36 more individuals implanted with the Medtronic stimulator. It's just the first stage of what they call *The Big Idea* — a bold, forward-thinking plan designed to find and follow the quickest path toward getting the stimulators further tested and approved for clinical use.

The issue, not surprisingly, is finding the money to make all that happen. Normally when new drugs or devices come on the market, it's because they hit a stage of development where some company can see profit on the horizon. That's hard to achieve with the stimulators, precisely because actually restoring function after paralysis is such uncharted territory.

And yet we know that the current version of the stimulator *already* works well enough that people in chairs are eager to get implanted; the last time I checked there were more than 4,000 names on the list of people hoping to be included in the next study. And not one of those guys implanted in Louisville has said, "Get this thing out of me." Quite the opposite. They're saying, "Wow, am I lucky!" For them, the "small" changes in function are enormous.

So, yes. There are lots of people who don't care if it's a Model T. They don't care if something much better is just a couple of years away. *They want it right now.* There are paralyzed people demanding that their regular doctors buy one of these things from Medtronic, get hold of someone from the Louisville lab for instructions, and just put the darn thing into their backs. Scientists have told me they're pretty sure there are doctors who have already done this, even though they have no way to figure out where it belongs or how to set it up properly.

Christopher Reeve, I realize, might be just a name to some of you. He was a movie star. He was an amazing, warm, intelligent human being. Right at the top of his career he got the worst possible kind of spinal cord injury, and it finally killed him about 10 years later. While he lived, he was nothing if not fierce about the urgent need for a cure. I have to think that if he were still around, he'd be livid at the slow pace of progress around the epidural stimulator.

That's how badly their patients want it.

The Big Idea isn't just to hand out a few dozen stimulators to lucky people like winners on a cheesy TV game show. It's a careful program meant to ramp up the demand for better devices by showing the world how reliably the Model T version works and how eager we are for even the smallest measure of regained function.

I know a lot of women who are partnered to men with spinal cord injuries. Some of them are doing okay. They've learned to cope with all of it. Their husbands and boyfriends are reasonably healthy, meaning they have jobs and hobbies. They're not going to the hospital every other month. But there are others — so many others — who struggle just to keep going. By far the biggest issues I hear about have to do with the bathroom and the bedroom. This is what they name when they're fantasizing about getting to a better place:

> If he could just pee. Seriously, if he could just do that one thing. If we didn't have to screw around for an hour with the stupid bowel program. Oh my God. I'm so tired of trying to figure out how to do sex. I don't even care about it, but he does… he does.

If Rob Summers got the ball rolling in such a way that there was government funding for a few more patients, what would happen if CDRF could produce dozens more? The Big Idea is that if the government can't fund this middle step, and companies won't fund it, the community is going to have to. Our friends at CDRF have placed a bet on us. They took a chance that enough of us were paying attention and more than willing to both contribute and spread the word.

There's another factor at play here. It should be obvious by now that rehab is going to be a big part of any recovery scheme, and that definitely includes epi-stim. We're going to need recovery centers — gyms that are staffed with people trained to help us and equipment designed to make standing and stepping possible. The 36 people who eventually get implanted in The Big Idea project will have to have places to work out… and if all goes well, so will hundreds of thousands of others as this technology becomes a reality for the rest of us.

There are some facilities like that now, scattered around the USA and the rest of the world. CDRF has formed what it calls the NeuroRecovery Network, a collection of 13 clinics where both therapy and research can happen; probably the 36 patients they implant with the Medtronic stimulator will be spending serious quality time in those facilities. With luck, we'll soon be looking at a rush to build more of them.

Here's one story that gives me hope.

One of the last things President Bill Clinton did before he left office was to sign the law that created a new "institute" at the National Institutes of Health (NIH). The NIH definitely deserves its own chapter, and it's going to get one. For now, I just want to talk about the piece of it that was born on December 29, 2000, when President Clinton signed that bill into law.

I'm talking about the National Institute of Biomedical Imaging and Bioengineering, fondly known as NIBIB. We care about the people there, because this organization did respond to success in human epidural stimulation trials. The people at the NIBIB didn't make the trials happen; the organization didn't even exist when most of the preliminary animal work was being done in the '80s and '90s. But the director of NIBIB saw, heard, and reacted. With good news staring him in the face, he didn't sit on his hands.

The story of how that happened illustrates some of the ways that we — the patient community — have already had an impact and could easily take things even further. Like so many other parts of the epi-stim tale, this one involved a bit of good luck.

See, the NIBIB held its 10th anniversary celebration in June of 2012, about a year after the Louisville team published their paper about Rob Summers. He had been in the news a lot that year, appearing on CBS, ABC, CNN, and ESPN. There were feature stories in *The New York Times*, *The Wall Street Journal*, and the *Los Angeles Times*. Rob had been bio-engineered, and the audience at the 10th anniversary celebration wanted to hear him in person.

The lucky part for us is that Rob happens to be a marvelous public speaker. He was in the just-before-lunch sweet spot during that day's agenda, and he pretty much stole the show. Dr. Reggie Edgerton, who was in the room that day, told me that Rob ignored his scheduled time slot and spoke for about 45 minutes. I can only imagine how compelling he was in that setting; I spent an afternoon with Rob recently, and I can testify that he's a natural.

It didn't have to happen that way. The first person to get one of those devices could have been a mumbling introvert with a fear of public speaking. Fortunately for us, that wasn't Rob.

All he had to do was tell them what had happened to him, beginning with the early morning hit-and-run in his driveway and ending with how it felt to realize that the stimulator was working far, far better than anyone had expected. Dr. Rod Pettigrew, the NIBIB director, was impressed. As a direct result of Rob's presentation, Reggie Edgerton and others were invited to do a presentation for the NIBIB Council.

The Council is the group that makes final decisions — after a long, involved vetting process — about which projects get funded and which don't. They set the priorities. During the presentation to the Council, Reggie mentioned that there were definitely going to be lots of angry people if something this promising got pushed to the back of the line. Dr. Pettigrew, who had been the recipient of many excited emails. from people in chairs, believed him.

We do have influence. We just need to exercise it.

PART FOUR

A HEALTHY ENVIRONMENT

17 GROUND ZERO

On the night a doctor told me my husband had broken his neck, I was just pathetically ignorant. I sat there on a grimy little couch just outside the ER waiting room and stared at the man as if he'd turned into a white-coat-wearing alien.

What was he talking about? Spinal cord injury? Bruce couldn't be paralyzed. He had stuff to do. He'd gone skiing that day, and he was a great skier — careful, strong, and graceful. It was impossible.

Gradually as the hours passed, the truth sank in and brought me to my knees. I remember the next morning, when one of our frightened girls asked me when Daddy would get better and come home. I poured her cereal and told her that it depended on how bad he was hurt. Maybe, if only a little of his cord was damaged, he would somehow be okay. Maybe there were, like, *degrees* of this thing.

As all of you certainly know by now, that's exactly the case. There are infinitely many kinds of damage to the cord, and nobody can tell what any of them mean in terms of function. Sometimes a C6 injury means your fingers are useless. Sometimes it means they only work on one of your hands. Lots of spasticity, or hardly any. A little neuropathic pain, or a nightmare of life with super-sensitive skin. There's no predicting. The not-really-alien doctor told me what turned out to be some wrong things that night, based on his examination of Bruce's MRIs. But like me, he didn't really have any way to know how bad the damage was.

I wonder sometimes if ER doctors ever get to follow up with the patients they see — if they ever talk to people like us to find out if their predictions were right. An MRI of an injury site is just a black and white image of the cord and the bones around it. The cord flows through dark nuggets of bone like a pale gray river, and if you know what you're looking for, you can

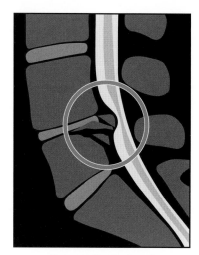

Damaged spinal cord

see the place where the river seems oddly pinched. You can see that the bones are cracked or jarred out of what had been their stony little path.

That's the spinal cord injury site as it's first examined after a catastrophe — a two-dimensional picture that means something terrible has happened. What is going on in there? At the level of the cells that make up the river, what exactly is happening?

I said this back in Chapter 3 about the star-shaped cells called astrocytes:

> *After an injury, astrocytes produce molecules that essentially build a wall around the damaged bit of the cord, and that's the only thing that prevents the entire cord from becoming one giant injury site. It's not the same as when, for example, you break your leg. The break in your leg is not going to spread from the point of fracture up into the bone above or below. It's going to hurt, and it's going to need to be repaired, but the damage is whatever it is, confined to the original break.*

In a spinal cord the injury site is ground zero. If those astrocytes didn't build that wall, the damage would spread and spread, like radiation after the explosion of an atom bomb. You might remember that the molecules that make up the protective wall are usually called CSPGs (because their actual name is kind of a mouthful). CSPGs are made of a core protein molecule that has chains of sugar molecules hanging off it. It's like a very spare and dried-up Christmas tree.

So that's one thing we know about the injury site. It's surrounded by a protective barrier of molecules. Any time something bad happens inside the brain or the spinal cord, astrocytes are going to rush to produce a ton of CSPGs that will form a wall. Inside that fortress, where there used to be a tangle of functioning axons and astrocytes, there will be more CSPGs. Lots of them.

What else is in there? Strangely, there will also be a whole population of oligodendrocyte precursor cells. Remember them? The vice-presidents that can only become wrapper cells. It turns out that there are a few of them in the brain and the cord all the time, apparently in case a regular wrapper cell dies. And just like the CSPGs, these precursor cells proliferate and show up in force after any kind of injury to the cord. There must be a chemical signal in the system that says it's going to be needing myelin soon.

Unfortunately, the vice-presidents don't get a signal that tells them to finish developing. They don't turn all the way into wrapper cells once they get to the injury. They just crowd in there with all the CSPGs, combining to form a sort of biological soup.

So there was my husband. He had plenty of healthy neurons up in his brain with millions and millions of axons descending into his cord. And right at the place where his vertebrae had shattered, some of those axons were stopped dead. They ran into the biological soup made of CSPG molecules and precursor cells but decided to stick around. Why?

Let's think about life from the perspective of an axon. There it is, coated in cozy myelin, falling gracefully down through the brain stem in big bundles with all its neighbors. Those bundles form the white matter on the outside perimeter of the cord, but the white matter is just the road. It's the river you see in the MRI. The destinations of every one of those axons are deep inside the cord, in the gray matter.

Inside the gray matter, they're home. Waiting for them there are what they've been aiming at: dendrites extending from the cell bodies of other neurons. When the far end of an axon from one nerve cell connects cleanly to a dendrite from another nerve cell, we get communication through the cord. Together, billions of times per second every day of your life, partnered cells are forming what's called a *synapse*.

Synapse comes from a Greek word that means "to clasp," but that's not a good description of what actually happens. There's really an impossibly tiny gap between one axon and another, about as wide as a human hair split 20,000 times. The gap is called the *synaptic cleft*. No clasping is involved; the nerve cells never touch.

What happens instead is that the tip of the axon is sending out tiny molecules called *neurotransmitters* into the gap. Those molecules are sort of like Lego pieces looking for the right match. On the receiving end, the dendrite is producing molecules called *receptors*. The receptors are the matching Legos. When a neurotransmitter crosses the tiny gap and slots into the waiting receptor, the chemistry of both of the nerve cells changes. That's how all

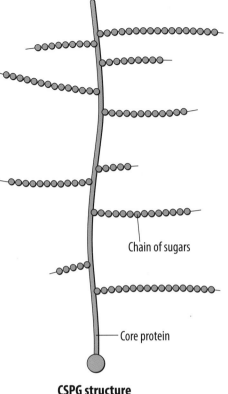

Chain of sugars

Core protein

CSPG structure

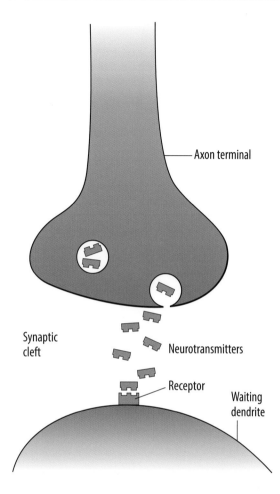

Axon terminal

Synaptic
cleft

Neurotransmitters

Receptor

Waiting
dendrite

information moves through your system. Hunger, pain, bending, flexing, thought — everything comes from tiny neurotransmitters docking into tiny receptors.

So what about those post-injury axons? Not that long ago it was common knowledge that axons dried up and died when they hit the injury site. That phenomenon was known as "Wallerian degeneration," named after one Augustus Waller, the British physician/scientist who first wrote about it in the 1850s. The common knowledge is turning out to be not quite right, though. Above the injury site, the axons are not dead, like dry broken branches dangling from a living tree. They're dormant. Sleeping. *Stuck.*

It really makes no sense for a live axon coming from a perfectly healthy neuron in the brain to just hang out endlessly in the cord's white matter, where there are no dendrites. Like all living things, axons follow a set of careful, precise instructions. The axon's goal in life is to form a synapse, so it's deeply weird that it would just stop somewhere and hang out indefinitely. Why would a healthy axon do that? What's trapping it?

And more importantly, how can we coax it into moving on? That's the subject of this part of the book: moving past ground zero. Getting axons to grow through the injury site is the approach scientists call *regeneration*.

18 Clearing Brush

If only bundles of axons *did* behave like broken legs. You'd just wear a cast for awhile, they'd knit back together, and presto. No more injury. What happens instead is that the little pocket of damage gets surrounded by CSPG molecules with their bristles of sugar chains. One of the scientists who's been working doggedly on how to repair spinal cord injury for his entire adult life has a helpful way to think about what's going on. His name is Dr. Jerry Silver, and he runs a lab at Case Western Reserve University in Cleveland, Ohio. Jerry's cartoon drawings of the situation are simple to understand and impossible to forget. The drawings show four different potential reasons why those axons get stuck; this is one of the areas where respected researchers disagree, which means that a lot of work still needs to be done.

Each cartoon is a simple line drawing that could be taken from a child's book: blue skies, yellow suns, green hills. In each frame is also the image of a neuron, with its fat cell body and long axon tail. In the first sketch, the neuron cell body is sitting on a hill (representing the healthy brain). Its axon reaches across the land toward an impenetrable red brick wall, where the terminal end lies hopelessly, apparently having smashed and broken. It would go on if it only could, but the wall prevents it. That wall represents the physical scar made of CSPGs. We can call this theory the *glial scar* hypothesis, because the astrocytes that produced those CSPGs are sometimes called *glial* cells.

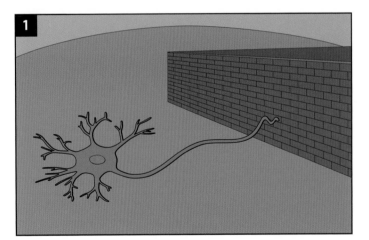

Cartoon series adapted from Jerry Silver's work as presented at Working 2 Walk 2012, Irvine, CA

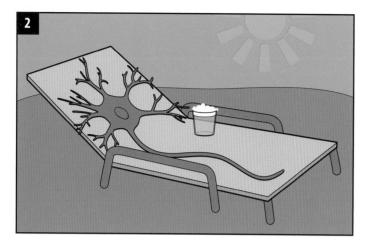

Picture number two shows a neuron draped over a beach chair under a bright yellow sun, taking its leisure and enjoying a foamy drink. The beach chair represents something that the axon likes; in this representation, growth doesn't stop because something *prevents* it. Growth stops because the axon has found a comfy spot — a sort of oasis — and it prefers to stay.

In possibility number three our axon has stopped at the rim of a deep gorge with a thin stream of blue water far down at the bottom. The axon could maybe grow across to the other side, but the gorge is deep, the gap wide, and the cell body too old and tired to make the effort. The gorge represents the hole in the cord. The river, too far away at the bottom, represents unreachable growth factors — vitamins that the tired neuron cell is lacking.

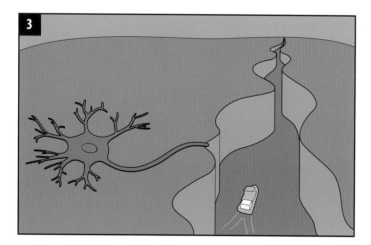

Drawing number four shows our axon at the edge of a wide blue lake. Swimming in that lake are sharks, crocodiles, and evil-looking red monsters; these all represent just what they sound like: *danger*. There could be molecules inside the glial scar or the cavity that are unfriendly to axons.

All the images could represent some piece of the reality our axons are facing, but it's taken decades of careful science to begin to figure out what it all means in terms of regeneration.

Okay, so let's take these pictures one at a time. If the goal is to clean up the environment at the injury site so that axons can get safely through, and if we know the names and addresses of what's in the way, it should be possible to fix this situation. Right?

Actually, a lot of that work is already done.

We'll start with the big red wall of CSPGs, the dried-up Christmas tree things, each one made of a strand of protein with chains of sugar molecules sticking out. Those sugar chains, it turns out, are what axons can't stand. The protein part of a CSPG is fine with them. In fact, so are most of the sugar chain branches on that little tree. Scientists have identified the baddest guy of the bunch, a sugar chain known as CSST 4,6. That particular chain is like axon-repellent, especially when the ratio of the different kinds of sugar chains is out of balance. The tree must be arranged just so, it turns out, in order for the axons to be happy. After injury, the balance is out of whack.

Great, so we know the names of the molecules and the structure that needs to be changed. What can we do about it? We're talking about something that exists deep inside the cord. When researchers study these things they're looking at dishes and slides of chemicals and cells under massive magnification. Finding ways to deal with CSST 4,6 in that kind of setting — intense as that is — doesn't begin to compare with getting rid of it in a living cord.

The best tool so far is an enzyme called *chondroitinase* (kun-DROY-ten-ace). You'll almost always see it called chABC, or Ch'ase. An enzyme is a particular kind of protein — the kind that makes chemical reactions happen faster. It's a catalyst, a thing that sparks change. ChABC is sort of a blunt tool for getting rid of the Christmas trees; it doesn't only attack the damaging sugar chains, it wipes out the whole tree.

At least, in lab animals it has done that. It has done that reliably in injured mice and rats for more than a decade, but it hasn't ever been tried in people living with paralysis. In 2013 I was at a conference about spinal cord injury research where a scientist named Dr. Marc Bacon spoke. He had a slide, I remember, that showed a long, long list of papers that showed how effective chABC has been in the lab. And he said this:

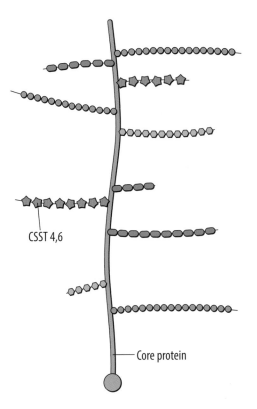

Chondroitinase is robust across models and labs. There's a wide therapeutic window, and there's a broad mechanistic effect. We should have taken it to the clinic a long time ago.

Working 2 Walk 2013, Boston, MA

The "wide therapeutic window" language means that chABC has been effective in lab animals not just right after injury but also later, in the chronic phase. "Robust" is the word scientists use to talk about results that are impressive — not a weak, hard-to-perceive improvement but one that's clear, reliable, and strong. The animals that got chABC got better. Marc was saying, "People, we've had this thing working in rats for a long time. We should be testing it in patients already!"

Why has that not happened? Well, it finally is. Almost. Sort of.

Later I want to talk about the money/inertia/regulatory reasons for it taking so long. Those reasons are real, and just as important to us as the state of the science itself. For now, though, let's stay focused on the science. What has prevented chABC from being ready for human use?

First, we'd have to have a pure and reliably safe supply. ChABC comes from bacteria. It's not a man-made enzyme, in other words; it's secreted by a little bug called *proteus vulgaris*. That bug lives, among other places, inside your intestines and mine. In bad cases of urinary tract infection, *proteus vulgaris* can contribute to the production of stones. So scientists will have to be able to show that the enzyme they plan to use in us has been harvested in such a way that it's known to be safe. It won't be enough to just say that it doesn't seem to have harmed any of the lab animals.

> One thing that I've heard people ask a lot is why it's not possible to simply cut the scar away — clean it out, so to speak, like you would if you ran across a bad spot when you were peeling potatoes. There are two reasons. One is that every millimeter of surviving cord is precious, so you wouldn't want to jeopardize the health of what's left. The other is that in some ways you'd just be re-creating the injury, and astrocytes would react by building a whole new CSPG wall. It would never end.

Another issue is that chABC doesn't last long at the temperature of the human body. It loses almost all of its ability to chew up CSPGs within a couple of days, but the astrocytes in our central nervous systems are very determined about making sure that the big red wall is in place. And that means going to one or more of the following approaches:

1. Multiple injury site injections over a period of weeks.
2. A temporary internal pump of some sort delivering the product to the injury site.
3. A way to keep chABC "fresh" for longer than a couple of days.
4. A whole different plan, maybe with something that attacks only the sugar chains.
5. Some other way to get chABC into our bodies, which will be discussed in chapter 20.

The first two possibilities on that list are a problem because *anything* that interferes physically with the cord is dangerous. There's always a real chance of doing more damage, right?

The third item on the list is being worked on, in the form of a molecule found in lots of plants but not in humans. It's called *trehalose*, and if you've ever been in the desert while rain was falling, you've witnessed it in action. Plants that looked shriveled up and dead before the rainfall are suddenly plump and healthy after-wards. The trehalose in those plants' cells protects important proteins from the effects of heat, and as it happens it does just the same thing for chABC in the toasty temperature of the human body. Trehalose plus chABC can destroy the big red wall very effectively — in lab dishes, anyway — for up to a month.

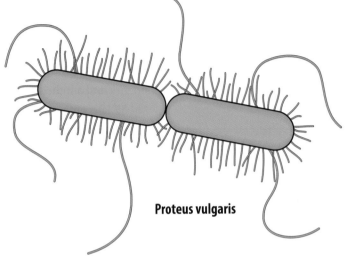

Proteus vulgaris

The fourth option makes my head start to hurt, because by now it's obvious that any new approach will certainly have issues of its own. We *really* don't want to go back to square one. I'm saving the fifth possibility for just a few more pages.

That's what we have for the first cartoon in terms of breaking down the CSPG wall and giving axons a chance to grow past the injury site. There are two pretty interesting ways that chABC is being tested right now, but neither of them involves us, or at least not directly.

One is at a veterinary medical center at Iowa State University. You might be surprised to know that dogs get paralyzed fairly often — so often that it made sense to do a dog version of a small clinical trial that combined an injection of chABC with state-of-the-art physical therapy. It's kind of brilliant, this trial.

Here's the study design:

1. Recruit a total of 60 dogs that have spinal cord injuries. The dogs need to have been unable to walk for at least six weeks, and their owners need to sign them up. (Facebook has been very helpful with recruitment!)
2. Anesthetize each dog and scan their spinal cords to get an image of their injuries.
3. For half the dogs, inject chABC doctored with trehalose into the injury sites. The in-jections go through the skin and into the dogs' cords, so there's no need for surgery.

19 THINK LIKE AN AXON

We can deal pretty quickly with the cartoons that have to do with the deep canyon and the lake full of monsters. The canyon symbolizes scarcity of nourishment. The picture implies that the neuron is *willing* to send that axon out across the injury site, but it's just too pooped. It needs a boost — some growth factors, or, to say it like the scientists do, *neurotrophins*.

What is it that makes an axon grow toward a target in the first place? It's got to have some sort of guidance, right? The process can't be completely random, and it's not. The targets are in charge. Target neurons in the brain and spinal cord produce tiny molecules that attract axons; they keep doing that until they've formed as many synapses as they possibly can. Those tiny molecules are the growth factors. They're like flashing signals that say, "Over here!"

After all of the necessary synapses are in place and that little bit of the larger system is functioning, the target cell will stop spitting out any more neurotrophins. It's as if a *No Vacancy* sign went up; axons will not grow toward that target anymore. It's not, as the cartoon suggests, that the neurons are too sick and tired; it's that the thing that would give them a reason to go forward isn't there. So, the thinking goes, if we want to coax axons across the chasm, we need to lure them with the same thing that motivated them in the first place: a nice, tempting growth factor.

If only it were that simple.

We know the structure of several important growth factor molecules, and scientists have been trying to use them to make paralyzed rats better for a very long time. Rats with thoracic injuries, cervical injuries, transections, hemisections, bruises, compression injuries — you name it — have been treated with growth factors. But all by themselves, those neurotrophins have not worked very well. Sometimes the rats will recover a little bit of movement, but there have been experiments where even that doesn't last. They actually lose that recovery again within a few weeks.

It's likely that when the day comes that we have a full, complete, back-to-normal cure, those tiny come-and-get-me molecules are going to play some part in it, but at this point they're like machine pieces we know will be good for something, just not exactly what.

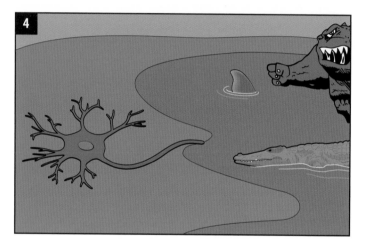

What about the lake full of monsters? Some of those monsters represent living cells that routinely show up whenever there's a trash collection problem inside the body. Got a paper cut? Within a day or so that injury site will be full of little garbage eaters called macrophages (MACK-row-fahjjez). When there's damage to the bundles of axons in your arms and legs, macrophages will rush to the scene and eat up things like bits of myelin and anything else that's lying around getting in the way of regeneration. After that, they go into an activated state and spit out molecules that act like growth factors, which is one of the reasons nerves in the arms and legs can regenerate. In the spinal cord macrophages do eat up debris, but they don't get activated. They don't spit out growth factors. They do, unfortunately, contribute to the inflammation that can kill off more cells than the original injury.

There are also molecules in that lake — not living monsters but more like tiny spanners thrown into the works. These molecules are usually called *inhibitory factors* because they stall or inhibit axons that are trying to make it across the injury site. Scientists identified the first one in 1994, and it was something of a shocker. The molecule's name gives away the surprise: *myelin-associated glycoprotein* (MAG, for short) is part of *myelin*. Yes. The very same stuff that makes communication between one neuron and another possible *also* makes it very difficult for axons to regenerate after an injury.

What is MAG doing in myelin? It turns out that for a new, young, baby axon, MAG is neutral — just part of the structure of myelin. But later, after an axon has matured, it's a major staller. It makes sense, right? We want axons to grow toward targets, form networks of synapses, and then focus on communicating. It would make no sense to have a system that didn't know when it was complete. So, having MAG molecules conveniently placed right there in the myelin wrapping is — from the healthy axon's point of view, a great idea.

MAG has friends, too, including another myelin-based molecule called, appropriately, *Nogo*. The strategy with these kinds of barriers is to find ways to neutralize them that don't do damage to the myelin, which of course we need. It's a very tricky problem, but not one that can't be solved.

So, where are we with the project of getting axons growing again? We have chABC that breaks down the red wall of CSPG molecules. We know the placement and structure of both important growth factors and critical inhibitory molecules. We know a lot about macrophages. The ultimate goal is to coax some surviving axons to cross the injury site and form new, useful connections with the healthy neurons below. We already know that in order to get meaningful recovery, every single axon doesn't have to make it over. Scientists assure us that this is true, and I personally know they're right because I've seen the MRIs that show the physical damage to my husband's cord.

They're terrifying. They're why that trauma center ER doctor told me not to be hopeful.

Bruce's cord goes from fat to almost nothing to fat again, but here's the thing: his injury is incomplete. He has a lot of working muscles. He gets around with a pair of canes. And that means that if it's possible to get even a small number of dormant axons back in business, many lives will be dramatically changed.

We're down to the last of the cartoons, the one that suggests the axons have found something they like in the injury site. Under this theory, they stay because for some reason it feels like home.

One of the very few human trials for spinal cord injury involved putting "activated" macrophages into the cords of 26 people with complete acute injuries. It didn't work; in fact, the 17 control patients (who got no treatment) were **more** likely to recover function than the ones who did get treatment.

We believe that it's this cartoon that represents what's really going on in spinal cord injury. The axons are happy because they've made a connection with an unusual cell in the lesion, and they persist for the rest of your life.

Jerry Silver, Working 2 Walk 2012, Irvine, CA

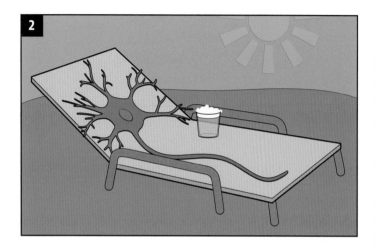

That was Jerry Silver, the person who drew these four cartoons a quarter of a century ago in an effort to capture all the possible reasons why the axon of a perfectly healthy neuron might not be able to grow through a lesion. (*Lesion* is what scientists call the injury site. It comes from a Latin word that means *to injure*). Jerry's lab unlocked the secret of the beach chair a couple of years ago; his team has been going full steam ahead to sort out the details ever since.

Here's what they figured out. Remember how I said at the beginning of this section that the injury site was a sort of biological soup? Oligodendrocyte precursors (the vice-president cells) and CSPGs (the Christmas tree molecules) are in that soup. And it's the combination of those two things that draws the axon in and convinces it to stay. The secret is that the tips of the growing axons — called growth cones — form what *feels* to them like a synaptic connection in that soup. It's not a real connection. It doesn't do anything. But from the axon's perspective, something that resembles a synapse is happening, and so they are as good as trapped.

The delicious foamy drink, so to speak, is a specific protein molecule — a special, sticky receptor that sits on the growth cone of the axon. When that receptor comes in contact with all those CSPGs, two things happen. One is that the receptor binds to the CSPGs, and the other is that the precursors get activated into a fake synapse mode. The growing tip of the axon stops right there, because this feels like home. One way to free the axons is the brick wall approach: get rid of the CSPGs. But what if we could forget the brick wall and make the receptors go away instead? The "stuckness" of the axons is a result of all three factors working together; the CSPGs, the precursors, and the receptors each play a part. What if there was a simple way to neutralize the receptors?

There is. It's called a peptide, which, by the way, is one of the few scientific names I like saying. *Peptide.* It sounds energetic and natural and strong. The peptide Jerry's group invented was just a simple enzyme known as ISP. It was designed to neutralize the receptors — to turn them off, in a way, so that they couldn't see the CSPGs. The idea is that if the peptide could neutralize the receptors, the axons would grow right past the injury site. Real synapses could be made below the site, and function would be restored.

Which is exactly what happened. Just months ago, at the very end of 2014, Jerry Silver's group published a new paper about the work they had been doing to push the peptide solution forward. Here are some highlights:

- 26 white lab rats were given spinal cord crush injuries, because that's the kind most humans have.
- All of them were given a plain old injection through the skin every day for the next seven weeks. The injection contained the peptide in a form that could get into the cord without the need to do surgery.
- 21 of those 26 animals recovered one or more of the following: bladder control, balance, or movement. Some got only one thing, some got two, and some got all three. *That's an 80% success rate.*

And that right there is robust evidence that the peptide is powerful stuff. Imagine what might happen when ISP gets used in a mix with growth factors, neutralizers of inhibitory molecules, chABC, and intense physical therapy. That combination would knock down all the cartoons.

That happy scenario leaves out one question, though, and it's something the cartoon with the tired old neuron trying to send its axon across the chasm suggests. What if the neurons have a sort of old age program built in? It could be the case that it's not just the brick wall and all the rest that has to be dealt with, but something in the axon itself that's saying, *"You're done. Don't regenerate."*

How would we deal with that?

20 CHANGING THE RULES

The question we've been trying to answer in this section is simple: *Why do axons in the spinal cord not regenerate after an injury, and how can we make them do that?* The last few chapters have been about things that are *in* the injury site but *outside* of the neuron cell, like missing growth factors and walls of CSPG molecules and tempting phony synapses. This chapter is about what's going on *inside* the neuron itself.

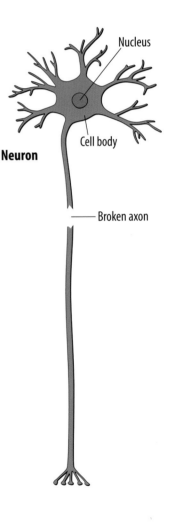

We have to start with your chromosomes. When I first started thinking about these things, I couldn't understand any of what I'm about to describe… I kept getting lost, because I'd have to look up the definition of each and every term, and by the time I got my head around the terminology I'd usually forget what the question was. As they say on the internet, I really needed someone to explain it to me like I was five. My last biology class was in 1968, and I remember it as a tedious series of exercises that led up to dissecting a dead frog. It wasn't inspiring.

When I finally *got* it I understood why it took scientists so many centuries to figure out even the most basic rules for how DNA works.

It's a very tricky process.

The structural part is pretty straightforward, though. Your chromosomes are tubular blobs of protein coiled around and around with a stringy sort of thing called DNA. DNA itself is just a very long (six feet when uncoiled!) molecule made of little sections called *genes*. That's it.

Most people have a total of 46 chromosomes that are arranged in 23 pairs. Chromosomes are named by their numbers, with Chromosome #1 being the biggest.

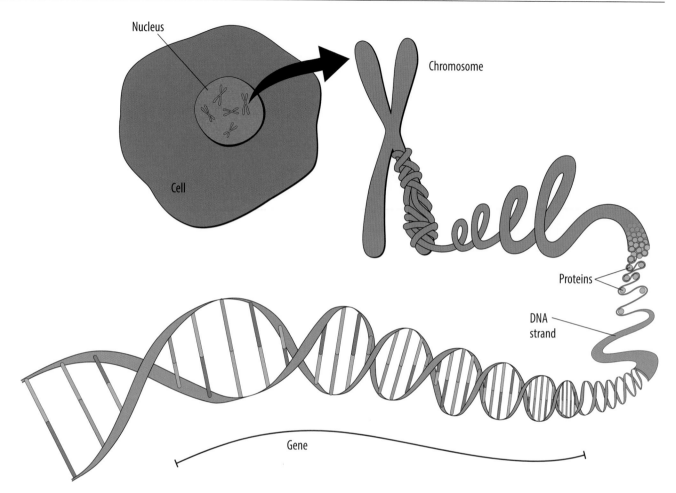

On Chromosome #1 there are more than 4,000 of the little segments known as genes. So far, so good. What's a gene, then, besides being a little hunk of DNA? *It's a recipe.* Genes are recipes for proteins. That's the secret. Every single gene in your system is a tiny code — a set of instructions for how to make a particular protein. The way those instructions get carried out really is marvelous, but we don't need to go down that trail. We just need to know that in a normal, functioning nervous system, the reason a particular protein enters the fray is because the gene that is its recipe is set to an *ON* position.

This matters in terms of axon regeneration because there was a time when your brain neurons were sending their axons down to form the tracts of your spinal cord. During gestation, that's what was happening. Axons grew. They must have had a signal at some point to stop growing, though, because that's what they did. And that signal would have been a protein of some kind.

And *that* means that if we know which gene is the recipe for that protein, we might be able to turn it back on. When you hear people talking about "gene therapy," this is one version of what they're trying to do:

- Figure out which combination of the 23,000 human genes creates a code for axons to grow.
- Build a little hunk of DNA with those particular genes set to ON.
- Use a virus to send that little hunk of DNA into the cells of a living creature, where it will reproduce itself.
- Watch to see if the needed proteins enter the system.
- Watch to see if damaged axons respond by growing.
- Test to see if the animal regains function.

Proteins are not living things, but they make it possible for us to live. They're antibodies against infection. They're catalysts. They're hormones. They're structural components. They make up about half the weight of most cells.

That would be a way to overcome the axon's built-in refusal to grow. Sounds crazy, right? That's what I thought until I met some of the people trying to make this happen for real. One of them is Dr. Os Steward, who directs the Reeve-Irvine Research Center in Irvine, California. He was part of a team that did that very procedure (on mice), targeting a gene known as *PTEN*. Because each gene is a recipe for a particular protein, it makes sense to call them by the same name. To avoid confusion, the gene is always italicized, and the protein that gene makes is not. So, the *PTEN* gene is the recipe for the PTEN protein.

Their theory was that PTEN was the protein that told neurons not to regenerate their broken axons. They managed to delete its gene — snip it right out of the DNA, sort of — and after that they did see axons growing through the injury site; they even saw some function being restored in those animals.

That was in 2012. Since then there's been slow but steady progress toward figuring out if this gene therapy idea can really work for us. When Dr Os Steward and his colleagues first did their mice experiments, they deleted *PTEN* and then gave the mice their injuries. Obviously that was never going to help us; they needed to show that if they messed with the gene after an injury they'd get the same result.

And, according to a paper published in April of 2015, they did.

Okay, not quite the same result. For reasons they don't fully understand, the axons didn't grow back in the same numbers they saw in the first studies, but hey — it's a start. When I read these papers I get a little dizzy… it's so exciting that someone has managed to rearrange the genetic code in such a way that axons can grow the way they did during gestation. And it's so frustrating that we're still at the mice stage, with an unknown number of years of effort in front of us.

The other recent news came from a team led by the scientist who gets credit for discovering back in 2008 what deleting *PTEN* might be able to do. His name is Dr. Zhigang He, he works at Harvard University, and his latest paper describes an effort to delete not just the *PTEN* gene but — simultaneously — another one.

Remember in Chapter 19 when we were talking about the injury site as a lake full of scary monsters and crocodiles that kept axons from safely crossing to the other side? I said that one of those monsters is a molecule called, appropriately, Nogo. What Dr He's team did was figure out which gene is the recipe for Nogo; then they knocked out that gene along with the one PTEN.

Good idea, yes? If axons can be freed up to grow as they once did and at the same time one of the barriers to their crossing can be neutralized, we could be in business. The experiment showed that it is possible to do both jobs at the same time; unfortunately the scientists did not see functional recovery. The mice couldn't move any better after the treatment than they could before.

Like I said, years of studies are ahead.

Os and Zhigang aren't the only scientists working the gene therapy end of the problem, either. Many others are exploring this direction, among them a young researcher named Dr. Murray Blackmore who hunts for these genes at his lab at Marquette University in Milwaukee, Wisconsin. So far he's identified three of them and is looking for more while his team tests these to see if manipulating them can lead to restored function. Murray is also the only scientist I know who's had a family member with a spinal cord injury — his mom became a quadriplegic when he was still a boy.

The good news about gene therapy is that it's both new and promising — an approach that's barely been explored at all, especially in spinal cord injury. We've only had a working draft of the human gene set (called the genome) for about 15 years. The bad news about gene therapy is the same: it's new, and there's a lot of work to be done before it becomes something we can use.

So, let's recap what we know about the "environment" of the injury. *What's going on, exactly, deep inside the cord where the damage is contained?*

There are broken axons, and for a whole host of reasons they don't grow past the carnage to form new connections. They've formed phony synapses, which trap them. They're confronting a pile of CSPG molecules, which stops them. They're missing the growth factors on the other side that would entice them to move along. They're confronting a set of dragons in the form of inhibitory molecules and macrophages. And finally — as if all that weren't bad enough — they have a built-in program deep in the genetic code that says: You're done growing. *Don't ever do it again.*

That's daunting.

When scientists first understood how the growth factors worked, they thought it was the answer. A breakthrough! Growing axons was going to happen. Paralyzed people were going to get better. That was in the late 1980s and early 1990s. A few years later the same thing happened with the inhibitory molecules. *Now we understand.* This time for sure, axons were going to grow. My husband's injury happened around then, so one of the first things I read about the cure was a trial in humans for an antibody to the Nogo molecule.

That trial began in the summer of 2006 and ended five years later; what had worked in injured animals didn't work in people — or at least it didn't work in the people they tested it on, in the doses they tested, during the timeframes they used. It's so important to get human trials exactly right, because failure might be for any of a dozen reasons.

What's amazing, in a way, is that so many scientists keep the faith. Take, for example, the people at the foundation called Spinal Research in the UK. Earlier I quoted their Executive and Scientific Director, Marc Bacon, saying publicly that the enzyme chABC should have been tested in people a long time ago. Since I heard him say that, Spinal Research has taken on that project, carefully building a case that will hopefully get chABC into people with spinal cord injuries for the first time.

It's Spinal Research money that's paying for the paralyzed dog study in Iowa: $200,000 has been invested in that project in the hope that results will convince regulators that the molecule is safe and effective and ready to test in people. It's also Spinal Research money that's paying for studies that will establish the safest way to deliver chABC into people. They've already set aside almost half a million dollars that's being spent in three closely cooperating labs. In the world of research funding, this isn't a lot of money. It is, however, a creative combination that could move things along more quickly. A therapy that works in dogs is a generally a lot more likely to work in people than one that works in mice.

Their approach is another twist on the gene therapy idea; instead of trying to change the don't-grow-axons instructions in neurons, they want to *add* the gene that is the recipe for chABC. If they can do it, that gene will make a person's cells produce chABC themselves.

If you're like me, at this point you're thinking that maybe regeneration is just too hard. Too many things in the way, too many possibilities for error, not enough reasons to believe it will ever work. When I start going down that road, I remind myself how many things seemed impossible right up until the moment somebody did them.

Part Five

In Their Shoes

21 Scientist Factories

My friend Roman Reed — who was paralyzed while making a tackle during a Chabot College football game in 1994 — describes the day that he confronted spinal cord injury science for the first time:

> My dad and I went to Stanford, and we went to the medical building. And we looked up spinal cord injury, and there's all these books, and we spent about $300, and we bought all these books. And we were determined. We were going to find a cure. And we read and read… and we looked at each other like, "Oh my God, what is this? Is this English? What IS this?" It became very apparent that I would never be the scientist who would find the cure.
>
> Roman Reed speech at Working 2 Walk 2012, Irvine, CA

It seems fair at this point to pay a little attention to the people who actually *are* the scientists finding ways to help us. What sort of people are they? How do they get into this field? What motivates them? These aren't idle questions; the more we know about how the world looks to them, the better we'll be as advocates. It's in our interest to get inside their shoes for a while.

Some of the places in the USA where researchers are focused on spinal cord injury

Spinal cord injury researchers are of course at work all over the planet, but for now I'm going to focus on the system that produces them here in the USA. That's only because the USA is where I am, not because we necessarily have figured out the best way to manage this process.

It also turns out that there's a simple analogy that captures our system, and it involves a very famous American.

When Benjamin Franklin was 12 years old, his father signed a contract that obliged the boy to spend his next nine years learning the trade of printing. The plan was that he would be under the supervision of a local master printer named James Franklin, who also happened to be Ben's older brother. Under the rules of the deal, Ben would move into James's home. He'd eat whatever James's wife felt like giving him. He'd be required to do all the menial work they felt like demanding. He'd be given no pay at all until the final year of the arrangement. If James wasn't satisfied with his attitude or his effort, he was free to beat Ben with any implements that came to hand. In fact, he was free to beat him for no reason at all.

Apprenticeship was thus a contract between the father of the boy apprentice and the master who took him on: room, board, and valuable training in a craft in exchange for submission, obedience, grunt work, and youth. It wasn't slavery, because there was an agreed-upon end point — but it wasn't just a job or a school either, because the apprentice wasn't free to leave.

" … to serve from the day of the date of these documents, seven years from thence following to be fully complete and ended. He shall serve, his secrets keep, his lawful commands everywhere gladly do; he shall not commit fornication; he shall not haunt taverns or playhouses; he shall behave himself towards his Master and all his Family… "

From a Standard Apprenticeship
    Agreement
Kenneth Spencer Research Library,
University of Kansas

If Ben survived the nine years, he would emerge into the printing world with the status of *journeyman*. He'd finally be able to earn wages working for another printer, but would not be allowed to open his own printing shop. For that he needed the status of *master*.

For many young men in the towns of colonial America, this system worked out fairly well. They learned, mostly, how to produce the kinds of goods that city-dwellers needed. Candles, soap, furniture, harnesses, shoes, carts, watches, ironwork — every trade had its secrets, and every trade took time to learn. Ben Franklin wasn't happy in his brother's home, though; his time under James's roof lasted only five of the promised nine years. At 17 he skipped out and ran away to Philadelphia, where his long and wildly productive career got underway.

The process by which a student becomes a scientist in the USA today has a lot in common with the old apprenticeship system — minus the beatings and some of the grunt work, and with slightly better pay.

The first step is a bachelor's degree, often but not necessarily in biology. I did a quick survey of the resumes of a few dozen top SCI neuroscientists this morning; they started out with bachelor's degrees in psychology, pharmacology, health and physical education, zoology, chemistry, and, yes, biology. Those degrees are the equivalent of a boy turning 12, in the scientist-making world.

Bachelor's degrees are the minimum point of entry. Today these degrees cost in the range of $70,000 and take four years to acquire, if the student is diligent and chooses a public university.

What happens next is the apprenticeship itself — the PhD program. Almost always, students choose to earn doctorate degrees because a working scientist whom they admire advises them to try it. Maybe there was a work-study job in a lab, or a random class where the instructor was also a researcher. Maybe there was an advisor who noticed an interest in the geeky side of life, or a family friend who suggested the possibility. Very few of them believe they're going to find a cure for paralysis, at least at the outset. The job is too big. One individual isn't going to be able to do it alone.

That said, many of the scientists I've met say that they turned to (and stuck with) spinal cord injury research because they were moved by specific people. It might have been the shocked parents of a teen with a broken back, or a family member of their own who was living with paralysis, or even someone in the news. This is important because it means that our very presence can be a powerful incentive. Simply being visible is part of what we have to do.

Whatever the motivating spark, the student makes a big commitment in choosing to work toward a PhD, and the scientist who agrees to supervise her work makes an equally big commitment in taking her on. It's very like the situation in which a new apprentice is brought under the wing of a master craftsman: the scientist is promising to train the student in a working lab; the student is promising to spend years doing the grunt work that's a big part of what we call science. The process is going to take several years. The student's work in the lab is the payment; the supervisor will benefit by getting a lot of "free" help on his own projects.

It's easy to see how important attracting great students is to the process, just as attracting high-quality apprentices would have been to a master's shop. The PhD supervisor isn't just training the student to use certain tools or design careful experiments or write coherent papers — he's preparing that student to take her place in a community of people whose work will eventually intersect with and build on her own. The apprentice expects to leave the master not just with skills but also with a reputation, connections, and and a high probability of getting the next job.

Competition to get into a PhD program is fierce, and our student will likely have to be willing to move. Labs will be at research universities, and the best ones are often on the coasts or in cities where living is expensive.

What does it cost to earn a doctorate? In biology and other life sciences, usually nothing. Most universities will waive tuition and even pay a small stipend as long as the student works in their labs, keeps up with class assignments, and makes progress toward her degree. Like the meals offered to apprenticed boys, the stipend won't be lavish. At Drexel University in modern Philadelphia, to take one example, a student in the PhD neuroscience program can expect a monthly check for about $1,900. She won't starve, but neither will she be able to start a family, buy a home, or travel. She's going to earn about as much as a full time Burger King shift manager. For five or six years.

Some dissertation titles on spinal cord injury make you wonder if the money spent is really going in the best possible direction. For example:

"Effects of sitting Tai Chi on sitting balance control and quality of life in community-dwelling persons with spinal cord injuries."

During those years, in addition to working in the lab, taking classes, and maybe helping to teach classes, she'll produce a fat document called a *dissertation*. The dissertation will be about her very own research project, which she'll have developed and carried out with help from her supervisor.

All of which is to say that getting a PhD to do spinal cord injury research is kind of an unusual undertaking in our culture. The people who take it on are generally not just bright — they're also disciplined, determined, extremely patient, and willing to sacrifice. They go into it knowing that it's going to take a long time; half the people who pull it off take *more* than six years to finish. And that means many of them are close to 30 by the time they're ready to take the next step.

Those who intend to stay in the world of universities — usually called *academia* — also know that there isn't going to be a big payoff in dollars later. Unlike, say, many people who become medical doctors, scientists will eventually make a good-but-not-extravagant living.

So, here's one thing we know so far: *our friends with PhDs working in university labs are highly unlikely to be motivated by personal wealth.* If they were, they'd have chosen to do something else. They have other kinds of goals. Something besides money is driving them.

Wherever schools have research labs, there are PhD candidates spending their time doing the grunt work of science, which is how I think about collecting data. Their most important job is to carry out the experiments exactly as they're designed and then measure, measure, measure every single detail of every single thing that happens. That collection of carefully gathered and recorded measurements become the data that leads to new insight and — always — more experiments.

If Ben Franklin had been the sort of kid who stuck it out and finished all nine years of his apprenticeship, he'd have been called a *journeyman*. He'd have been seen as qualified to earn a reasonable wage for doing highly skilled work in another man's print shop. In the academic world, a student who sticks it out and finishes all six-plus years of a PhD program is likewise ready to work for pay in another scientist's lab.

She'll have some basic skills in neuroscience. She'll know how to care for the white rats they like to use. She'll know how to section and stain slides, how to operate equipment, how to record and interpret results. She'll be able to use fancy mathematics, and she'll know where her projects fit into the big picture of similar projects others are doing around the world. She'll be capable of writing the articles that describe the experiments and the results.

What does all that get her? A job, hopefully. She'll be looking for what's called a *postdoc* position, where she can expect to spend a few more years of her life. She's become a journeyman.

Here's a current job listing in neuroscience at a prominent SCI-repair research center:

> *Positions for postdoctoral fellows… must have a demonstrated background in neuroinflammation and/or trauma and be familiar with microsurgery, live imaging (two photon microscopy experience is a strong asset), molecular and cellular techniques. Applicants must have a PhD (preferably in the last 2 years) or*

about to obtain a PhD in a related field (e.g. Neuroscience, Immunology, Cancer), and be eligible or currently hold funding.

Kentucky Spinal Cord Injury Research Center, September 2014

What does all of that mean? To work in this research center, she has to have done her PhD apprenticeship in a lab where there was a focus on how the spinal cord becomes inflamed after injury. She needs to know how to do surgery using extremely tiny instruments. She should have experience using a delicate and fabulously expensive kind of laser-based microscope that lets her look deeply into living tissue. She needs to know the biology of cells and the chemistry of molecules.

Her PhD has to be recent, because if more than a year or two has passed since she got it there will be new technologies and techniques that she won't understand. And finally, she has to bring money ("funding") into the lab with her. How does a scientist get funding? She writes what's called a "grant" — a detailed proposal about the sort of experiment she wants to do. It's a pitch.

A good grant will do a lot of work. It will convince the people who review it that the scientist has asked an interesting question. It could be an old question, like "How exactly do those CSPG molecules prevent axons from growing after a spinal cord injury?" or it could be a completely new question, but either way it must be an *unanswered* question. The grant will describe (in excruciating detail) the experiment that she thinks could answer that question clearly and surely. It will demonstrate that she's also thought about the possible ways the experiment might fail to answer the question. It will show what ways she's devised to prevent those failures, and it will make the case that she has the chops to pull the project off. *Some scientists spend as much as half their time writing grants.*

So, back to our new PhD, who is looking to get herself a postdoc position. She will need to either bring a grant along or be able to secure one quickly. If that seems backwards, it is — at least from the perspective of how jobs normally work. She's going to get paid, but she isn't going to get the job unless she can bring resources in the form of the ability to get grants into the new lab. It's as if a person couldn't get hired to write computer code unless a list of paying customers was included on his resume.

If she gets the job, her postdoc salary will be a big jump from her student-level stipend, but she'll be able to count on it only for a few years, at which point she'll need to make her next move.

She'll have only a few options, and all of them are going to be extremely competitive. She'll have to be very good, or have very influential mentors, or have access to funding that others don't, or have gotten very lucky in her work, or all of the above.

This matters to us.

It matters because we depend on these particular people — the PhD students and the working scientists they become — to focus on spinal cord injury research.

If they can't get through grad school because there aren't enough places for all the good applicants, we lose. If they can't find postdoc positions because there's not enough funding to get all the worthwhile grants approved, we lose. If there's no money to expand labs or build new ones, we lose.

Some fraction of those perfectly willing and qualified people will go off and do another kind of science or move into another profession altogether, and the work they might have been doing will have to wait until someone figures out a way to make it happen. When that happens, we lose.

At the beginning of this chapter, I quoted Roman Reed describing his realization that he personally was not going to be the guy who was going to figure out how to repair his own broken neck. What I didn't say is that his very next move was to figure out how to raise money to support the people he believed might be able to do it for him. If you ever get a chance, thank him for that.

fourth is — in terms of how big her investment so far has been — like sinking. It's giving up. Giving up on spinal cord injury research happens routinely, and at least some of the time it's a colossal waste of hard-won expertise.

The problem is that there are only so many labs to go around. Think about it. If there are ten labs in the USA doing deep research into spinal cord injury repair, and each of them is training two postdocs, that would mean that there would need to be twenty new jobs for those people within a few years. There aren't going to be twenty new labs, for sure. There might be one or two, and there might be a couple of retirements — but no way will all those qualified people move into their own labs.

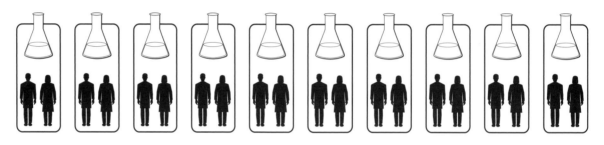

This is another piece of information we care about, for two reasons. One is that this means the people who *do* get their own labs are absolute superstars. They're literally one-in-a-thousand-quality scientists. The other is that we're looking at a big talent pool that's qualified and trained to help find treatments for spinal cord injury, but there is no place where they can do that work. *Unacceptable.*

So if two or three of our twenty postdocs get jobs in cutting edge spinal cord injury research, what happens to the other seventeen or eighteen? They're more than qualified to become staff in other peoples' labs, but remember that most of the time the work a staff scientist would do gets done instead by the postdocs and PhD students already there. Only big labs with lots of money can afford to keep paid staff, but big labs also are the likeliest to attract trainees who are bringing their own funding along, so why would they want to pay staff?

They wouldn't.

The situation for our postdoc is fairly dire. She's already spent $70,000 on her bachelor's degree. She's got a PhD and she's finished a couple of postdocs. She's over 30 and if she ever wants to do something radical like have a family or buy a condo, it's time to get a stable job.

Maybe she really, really wants to work in a research university, and if that's the case, she gambles. She takes a job as an untenured faculty member, and that's when the screws really start to get tight. She has only three years to prove herself worthy of becoming permanent faculty — sometimes only two years. During those years, she has to go out and find funding for her research. Her science has to work, because if it doesn't it won't get published. Her ability to keep her job depends almost completely on how many papers she manages to publish. And she has a teaching load at the same time.

And guess what? The way to get lots of papers published is not to take risks and think boldly. The way to get lots of papers published is to do careful work around the margins of what's already known. Our scientist is not crazy; she's going to do what she has to in order to keep her job. This situation is repeated about a thousand times every day of the week.

If she fails at any of these things — bringing in grant money, conducting successful experiments, or teaching effectively — she's toast. No job in science.

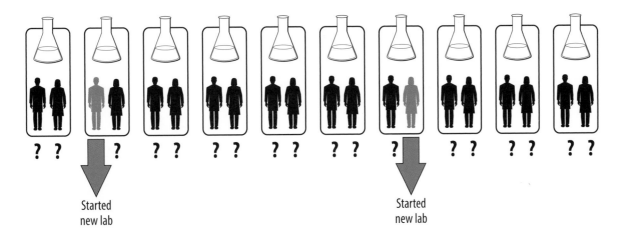

Started
new lab

Started
new lab

Recently I asked a friend who managed to make it through this system what seemed to me like an obvious question: *What's the point of training so many PhDs if there'll never be jobs for them?* And he told me something I hadn't understood. Universities get to keep a lot of the grant money that young scientists go out and get. The percentage varies from school to school, but it's very high. *My friend's school takes 62% of every dollar of his funding.* What that means is that our young neuroscientist — the person we're depending on to carry out the work that will result in therapies for us — is actually helping support *other programs* inside her university with the dollars she manages to bring in.

This situation got even worse when the recession began in 2007. By law, most states can't carry debt, and almost all of them lost boatloads of tax revenue when millions of people lost their jobs. So states had no choice but to find things to cut, and the universities took a big hit; nationwide, state support for college education dropped by 20%. The money to run the schools still has to come from somewhere, though, and that's one of the reasons for universities to suck up cash from science grants.

So, when the National Institutes of Health (NIH) writes a check for $100,000 that is supposedly paying for my friend's experiments, really only $38,000 of that amount will be spent on the science. The rest will be used to keep his college afloat, often in ways that have nothing at all to do with science. It's kind of mind-boggling — a sort of backdoor way to fund universities, riding on the shoulders of taxpayers through the work of PhD students and postdocs.

Keep this in mind when you read about how much money the NIH spends on research, and remember that most scientists are forced to spend as much as *half* their time writing grants in order to get that money. There has to be a simpler and more straightforward way to keep our universities running. There has to.

Since there are nowhere near enough university labs to employ them, most of the trained scientists who want to stay in the field will go to work in the private sector, where there are more options and where they can maybe enjoy some stability. Here's what their choices look like:

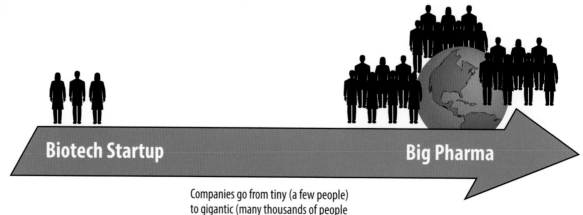

Biotech Startup　　　　**Big Pharma**

Companies go from tiny (a few people) to gigantic (many thousands of people spread across the globe)

An example of a nice, no-financial-worries place where our neuroscientist can find work might be Johnson & Johnson, which is the biggest pharmaceutical company in the world. J & J's income from its line of "Neuroscience Pharmaceuticals" in 2013 was $6.7 billion, mostly from sales of drugs aimed at schizophrenia and attention-deficit disorder. The skills and background our scientist acquired during her years studying the brain and spinal cord will make a job in the J & J labs doable. It would be like someone trained in Paris to be a master chef getting hired on as the soufflé-maker at Ruth's Chris Steak House. Steady, respectable work that not just anybody can do. The possibility of having a life. An end to the pressure of thinking up experiments, getting money to fund them, hoping they work, and frantically pushing to publish the results.

Just make the soufflés and go home. We can't be surprised that lots of postdocs do just that. In terms of our goal — *to get faster cures* — those people represent lost time and lost investment.

But what about the other end of the spectrum? Don't some scientists leave academia to start their own companies? Sure. The world of biotech startups, though, is a territory that's not for the faint of heart.

23 Just Start a Company

Before we get to the question of startups, let's take a minute to get a feel for what life is like for our academic lab scientist.

She has a promising idea about an experiment that will tell us something useful about damaged spinal cords and how to repair them. Great. It will take some money to test her idea, so she writes a proposal — called a *grant* — explaining what she wants to do and why she thinks it will work. Her idea has to be original. She has to convince the people with the dollars that she's got the chops to pull off what she's proposing to do.

So, that's where the whole process begins. And where does it end? Every time our scientist gets money to fund her next experiment, the goal is the same. Do you see it?

Her goal is over toward the bottom left side of the diagram: *Peer-Reviewed Paper Published*. Notice what it doesn't say? It doesn't say *Cure for Spinal Cord Injury*. Every scientist I've ever talked with does want to find a way to help us. They really do. But their day-to-day, month-to-month, year-to-year agenda is to publish papers showing their work. That's how they pay the rent and keep their jobs. That diagram really is a picture of how the world spins for most of the people doing actual science. It's an endless cycle of asking for money, trying to design careful experiments, hopefully getting results that matter from those experiments, and then publishing those results for all their peers to build on. Wash. Rinse. Repeat.

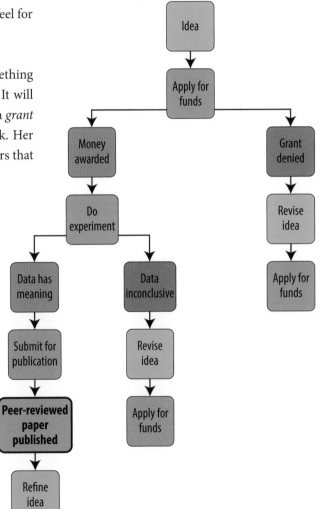

Each one of those bits can take a long, long time. Grant cycles can be once-a-year. Experiments can take two years, especially if they're done with chronic animals. Publishing can take a year or more, and that's after the time it takes to write the paper. If there weren't so many bright and dedicated people doing this, it would be discouraging.

Okay, that was irony. It *is* discouraging. It is discouraging to think of all those scientists cycling through the years, publishing papers and never getting much of anywhere.

So what happens if lightning strikes? What if our scientist actually finds something that could make life a little better for someone with a spinal cord injury? Suppose our talented postdoc is one of the special few who earned her own lab. Suppose that after twenty or thirty years of marching through the system I just described she has actually found something that will help people get some function back. She's done all the animal models and even shown that it works in a few humans.

It could be a type of cell, like the ones we talked about back in the second section of this book. It could be a device, like an epidural stimulator or an injury site scaffold. Or it could be a drug like those peptides or the enzyme chABC. Our scientist has been noodling over how to repair spinal cord injury for decades. She wants to see people getting better. She thinks it's time to take her product to market.

Yay, say we! *Bring it.*

Do scientists make good entrepreneurs? Sometimes. Okay, rarely. These diagrams illustrate one way to look at why.

We can all see the problem here. A lot of the qualities that make a person good at starting a company aren't naturally present in a person who's great at thinking up and carrying out experiments. It does happen once in a while, but it's just not reasonable

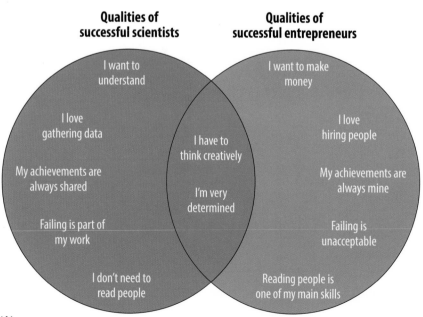

Qualities of successful scientists

I want to understand

I love gathering data

My achievements are always shared

Failing is part of my work

I don't need to read people

Qualities of successful entrepreneurs

I want to make money

I love hiring people

My achievements are always mine

Failing is unacceptable

Reading people is one of my main skills

I have to think creatively

I'm very determined

to expect that our friends in the labs are going to be inclined to leave those labs. They're there for a reason, after all.

We're going to suppose that a scientist did come up with a new way to relieve some of the issues that go with paralysis. What would happen next, in an ideal world? How does a success in the lab turn into something a doctor can order and that our insurance will pay for?

Recently a friend walked me through the process. Like so many things, it's all about the dollars.

Let's say I'm the scientist, and I've shown that GizmoDrug can restore the ability to pee *almost* naturally for all kinds of paralyzed animals and seven out of seven paralyzed people that I've tested it with. My human subjects are thrilled. No more catheters. No more UTIs. Great news. So who is going to get GizmoDrug into the drugstore or the doctor's office? I'm just a researcher, I don't know how business works.

I need a company to do this. So either I quit doing research and devote myself to making this company, or I find a partner. My partner could be some giant corporation who wants to take GizmoDrug over and make a pile of money off it, or it could be a friend who understands business, but it's probably not going to be me.

The best thing would be for an existing company to look at what I've done and offer to help. "Hey, that's a really important achievement, helping people be able to pee! We'd like to make sure you get that product to as many patients as possible. We want it to be part of our portfolio."

That isn't likely. Why not? Because most people who aren't paralyzed don't get how life-changing it would be to have that particular function back. They haven't wet their pants in public since they were two, and the memory is lost. If I went out looking for a company to get my GizmoDrug through the maze of steps that lead to the market, very few people would see its value. "It's not a cure," they would say. "It's not enough."

The reason they're so skeptical is that it costs a lot to get a product through the system, which means that existing companies don't want to do it if they don't see a big fat payback at the end. They'd rather somebody else pay for all that preliminary stuff so they can avoid spending any of their money until it's for sure that the product is going to sell. You can't blame them.

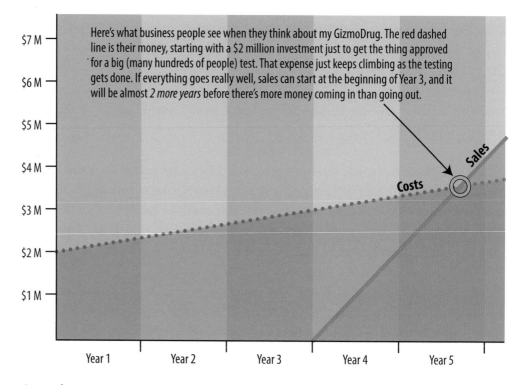

Here's what business people see when they think about my GizmoDrug. The red dashed line is their money, starting with a $2 million investment just to get the thing approved for a big (many hundreds of people) test. That expense just keeps climbing as the testing gets done. If everything goes really well, sales can start at the beginning of Year 3, and it will be almost *2 more years* before there's more money coming in than going out.

So, yeah. An existing company would prefer to come on that scene as late as possible — preferably close to the moment the green line starts. Where, then, will I get those red-dot dollars to get my product to that stage?

We've arrived at what's known as the *Valley of Death*.

It's called that because the answer is that there's no logical way to come up with that money — not for a product that's so important to us but so insignificant in terms of its eventual ability to make a profit. But let's say I'm not going to give up on GizmoDrug. I'm going to form my own company and try to make it to Year 3. Now what?

I need to license GizmoDrug from the university where I work. This is a sort of negotiation, where I approach them and say, "Hey. While I've been on the faculty here, I invented a new thing. It's technically your intellectual property, but you're not going to do anything with it, so how about licensing it to my new company?"

They will say, "Okay. We'd like a little money from your sales, please. After all, we've made it possible for you to discover this thing."

And we'll argue back and forth until we arrive at a number. They're going to get royalties for as long as the patent on GizmoDrug lasts, which is usually 20 years. Yes, I'll have to file for a patent, which will mean finding (and paying) a good lawyer. My patent will need to show that my product is different from anything else available, and it will need to be written in such a way that another company can't come along and tweak my product a little and then sell it as their own.

These things will take time — as long as a full year — and they'll be expensive. Once they're done, I can seriously start to ask for the money that will get me to Year 3. What I'm looking for is people or groups of people who see the value of the product and want to invest in it. *Invest* is the key word. They're not donors. They're not just handing out cash for the heck of it; they expect to get that cash back plus a healthy chunk more.

And that means that I need to have a business plan that will convince them that (a) lots of people really will buy this thing, and (b) they'll be willing to pay more than what it costs to make. Again, I'm a scientist. I don't know any investors. I've never been in a boardroom. I don't really understand business. All I know is that my product will help real people, and they should have access to it.

If I can't find anybody to invest in GizmoDrug, I'm dead in the water. I've mortgaged my house to pay for lawyers and worked double time for more than a year trying to line up the ducks in a nice neat row, but there's nothing I can do if I can't convince people with money that my product is worth making. I am not going to get to Year 3.

And if I don't get to Year 3, my discovery will never help anybody.

There are three kinds of investors. One is "angels," which is what we call individual people who hand over tens of thousands of dollars to startups. Another is groups of angels, who pool their money and decide together which startups to invest in. The last is venture capitalists, which are groups who have multiple millions of dollars to play with. All of them are looking for the big payoff. "Angels" sounds nice, but they want a good return just as much as the big guys do.

This, friends, actually happens. In fact, it very nearly happened with the spinal stimulator those Louisville scientists implanted in Rob Summers way back at the end of 2009. I just used an imaginary product called GizmoDrug to illustrate what it's like to be a researcher with a product that needs to get to market. Here's the actual timeline for the case of the spinal stimulator:

It starts with decades of lab work with animal models to prove the concept; Dr Reggie Edgerton, Dr Susan Harkema, Dr Gregoire Courtine, Dr Yuri Gerasimenko, and others have published multiple papers that clearly showed how safe and effective spinal stimulators were in rats.

The existence of the Medtronic pain device, its status as FDA-approved, and its documented record for safety in spinal cord-injured people made it attractive as a possible testing device — but those are the only reasons it was attractive. There was no real expectation that it would work; the scientists would have much preferred to develop a new device for their human tests, but the cost of doing that would have run into the hundreds of millions of dollars. This created a sort of chicken and egg moment… who would put that kind of money on the line without some sort of assurance that it would pay off?

Nobody. No one was interested, no matter how promising the animal studies were. And so the decision was made to implant Rob with a device that was understood to be a very crude approximation of whatever the final product would turn out to be. Rob's partial recovery of both autonomic function (sweating, urination, orgasm) and voluntary movement shocked everyone. If a crude device like the Medtronic one worked, what would happen when people with spinal cord injuries got stimulators engineered for their particular needs?

So, with that surprising success in hand, the scientists went back to the big companies, looking for partners to help them build a more sophisticated stimulator. No dice. Too much risk, too small a market, too far away from a profit. This is when NeuroRecovery Technologies (NRT) was formed, with Dr Reggie Edgerton as its Chief Scientific Officer. It seemed to be the fastest way to get the new devices designed, tested, and built.

The plan at NRT was to scare up enough money to build a working transcutaneous stimulator — a device that would have the same kind of effect as an implanted one, but without the need for surgery. Dr Yuri Gerasimenko, who is also on the company's scientific team, had already proved the concept in animals. The cost to produce it would be lower, and because no surgery would be involved the process of getting it through the FDA would be much simpler.

Everything hinged on finding the funds to get that transcutaneous product engineered and convincing the FDA to allow it to be tested in people. That's been done. NRT has a solid prototype of their non-invasive product. The regulators have given them permission to test it on volunteers. If it works, the next step will be to leverage that success into investment aimed at getting the implantable model perfected and tested.

The thing I want all of us to realize here is this: none of this was ever guaranteed to happen. The idea of spinal stimulators could easily have languished around for a few more years. As big a deal as it is to you and me, it was barely on the radar for investors and big pharmaceutical companies.

And once I get over being angry about that, I land on a couple of thoughts. One is that as long as our community is invisible and quiet, investors are not crazy when they assume that we don't exist and don't care about products that could help us. The other is that we all live on a sort of knife's edge. We have to figure out how to live with the injury, or we'll just drive ourselves crazy. But we can't let success at living with the injury translate into acceptance of the status quo. There has to be a way to do both — to live successfully *and* to push back against the idea that living successfully means we don't really care about cures.

PART SIX

GO FUND US

24 A Matter of Time

We need to talk a lot more about dollars. Euros. Yen. Pounds. Whatever it is that measures value and is always in short supply when it comes to research. I've just spent pages and pages describing the biological problem of repairing spinal cord injury. I've discussed the academic system within which research happens. Here a summary: A working central nervous system is massively complex; a broken one is even more so. Researchers are people who have to work their tails off for not much money, especially during the first 10 years after earning their PhDs. And only a tiny fraction of PhDs moves on to run their own labs. For all scientists, failure is the most likely outcome; many experiments end with ambiguous results, meaning nothing was learned. For a scientist, that's the definition of failure: *nothing was learned except what not to try next time.*

What we want to do is figure out how to make things easier for scientists. Why? Not out of kindness, though most of us are kind. We just want the people working on spinal cord injury to be more productive. Here's a representative sampling of things I've heard successful scientists say:

- *The research can only go as fast as the money comes in.*
- *All of us are struggling just to float our individual labs.*
- *More money would be the biggest improvement. With adequate time, the spinal cord injury field could easily tolerate a doubling or tripling of funding.*

All of those speakers are people with their own labs and lots of publications. They're leaders in the field — the one tenth of the one percent. What they never say — unless they're being ironic — is that they have enough money to do what needs to be done. That's because they don't.

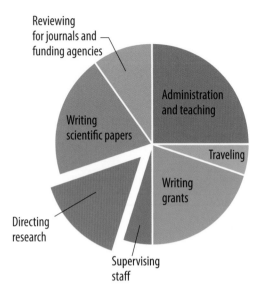

Reviewing for journals and funding agencies

Writing scientific papers

Administration and teaching

Directing research

Supervising staff

Writing grants

Traveling

Our friend Dr. Chet Moritz, who runs a very good SCI research lab at the University of Washington in Seattle, broke down his time for me this way: a fifth is spent writing the grants that will keep his team working. Another fifth is spent writing up results of work already done so that it can get reviewed and published. That's 40% of his time. Throw in some teaching, supervising and administrative duties, reviewing other scientists' articles, traveling to conferences, and meeting with collaborators at other universities, and 85% of his time is gone.

Obviously, a lot of research planning and evaluating gets done in the process of writing grants and papers. And scientific meetings are often where good ideas get exchanged. But if all that stuff is taking up 85% of Chet's time, he's got only six or seven hours per week to be in the lab directing the day-to-day research. So there's one very clear answer to the question of how to make the research go faster, right? Free up the scientists to do more, you know, *science*.

When I talked to Chet in late 2014 he had 13 people to manage, including staff, postdocs, grad students, and undergraduates. The space these people work in is like a small apartment: 800 square feet in three rooms. There are also always a few medical types (interns, residents, fellows) coming by to learn.

The cost to run that lab? Between $200,000 and $300,000 a year. This doesn't count the fellowships that he and his post-docs and grad students have to secure, so that budget is to pay Chet himself and his two or three full-time staff, and to buy equipment and supplies. He has to go out and find that money, which means convincing someone that he'll spend it well. As is typical in medical schools, the university isn't paying him much beyond his minimal teaching and administrative duties, and providing him a space to work.

So that's a reality. If Chet and all the others in his position could somehow spend less time chasing dollars, they'd be able to do more science. Faster science. More organized science. It doesn't seem like asking for the moon, to have a highly capable researcher be able to spend three or even four out of every seven working hours planning, directing, and evaluating research. Hold that thought.

Right now there are roughly 250 scientists doing spinal cord injury research in the USA, and they're almost completely funded by some combination of taxpayer dollars and nonprofit foundation grants. What are they doing? What are they spending all that money on? Some are doing basic biology, which involves things like figuring out which gene produces which protein, and what that protein is for, and how it interacts with other proteins. Basic biology is about the structures of molecules and the habits of cells. It's detangling the parts and processes that make up living things. Its only goal is to learn; there's no expectation of cures. Sometimes this is called *pure* science, probably because it's uncontaminated by any expectation of reward.

After basic biology comes investigation aimed at applications, which is why it's usually called *applied* science. Once you have enough of a feel for the parts, you can tinker with them, in lab dishes and in living creatures. What happens if I put some Schwann cells just above the broken part of a rat's spinal cord and give them a tiny nerve bridge to cross? How about if I do that with some growth factors? How about if I change the mix of the growth factors? What happens if I do this kind of rehab instead of that one after an incomplete injury?

Both basic science and applied science can be long-haul projects; in a way, they're *meant* to be endless. There will always be 20 new questions for every one that gets answered. Our system is set up not just to allow that, but to *encourage* it, which means that a whole lot of money gets spent not just to find facts but to lead to lots and lots of new questions. From a global, centuries-long point of view, this style of doing science really has proved to be a solid way to move whole fields of interest forward.

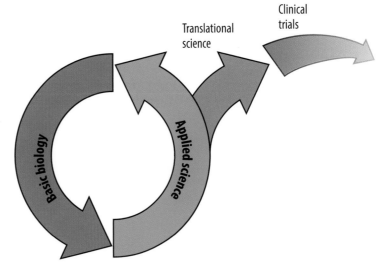

However. From an advocate's point of view — mine and yours, I mean — it pretty much fails. The larger system doesn't share our goal of finding ways to get back function as quickly as possible. Applied science doesn't care all that much about your neuropathic pain or my husband's useless right hand. It's focused on asking good questions and designing experiments that can answer them with authority. Scientists doing this kind of work aren't indifferent to our world at all… but they have to have a very narrow focus. That's why so much of the time it feels like what researchers are doing is competing with one another to spin the same irrelevant wheels. The wheels aren't irrelevant to them; the wheels are their job. They are learning new information, and we can't know in advance whether it will be helpful or not.

It would be unreasonable for any of us to storm their labs and demand that they stop doing what they're doing. It does make sense, though, to keep these questions in front of them: *What is the logical next step that follows from your investigation, assuming that it shows clear results? Where exactly does it lead?* If the answer is, back to the basic biologists so they can tease out more information, okay. We *can't* argue that more information isn't needed — but we can (and I think we have to) argue that basic biology shouldn't eat up all the available funding. We can ask the people who are handing out the money to keep those questions in the mix, and we can ask them to let us see the track record for what has moved forward, what it cost, and how long it took.

Okay. Suppose something really great happens, and an investigator finds out that this or that molecule or cell actually works in a dish or even in a mouse. Fantastic! We can move on to the third category in my personal set of science-type boxes, which is translational or preclinical research. *Translation*, in this context, means taking that early success and showing that there's reason to think it will work in people — that it will *translate* from the mouse to you.

It's called *preclinical* because the word *clinic* means hospital, a place where people go to get treated. Preclinical means *before the hospital* — before people. This kind of research involves working with lots of animals, and usually with more than one species. It involves super careful tracking and measurement and very cautious writing of results.

> The scientists I know aren't different from anybody else. They want to be right. They want what they're working on to turn out to be important. But they have to spend a lot of their time figuring out ways that they're probably wrong. As Dr. Murray Blackmore put it, "You try to disprove what you hope is true. You try to kill your own baby, and yet you want it so badly to live."

1989: *Mouse* neural stem cells are identified at a lab in Albany, New York.

1999: *Human* neural stem cells are first isolated at a lab owned by a Palo Alto company called StemCells, Inc.

Basic biology

1989

1999

In the time I've been paying attention, it used to be so rare that translational science in spinal cord injury actually got as far as trials in humans. I'm saying, almost nothing made it out of the labs and into even a few patients. Research stalls for lots of reasons. Sometimes it's because the early fantastic results couldn't be repeated, or because they didn't work reliably, or — worst case — because the scientist saw more in his results than was really there. It takes ingenuity to show that what you're claiming to be true is actually true. It also takes a whole lot of time and money.

Here's an example of what getting all the way to human trials looks like. I mentioned this story way back in Chapter 10, when we were looking at the different kinds of cells that may end up helping us.

This time, let's look at it from the perspective of money. The timeline only exists because a lot of somebodies handed over a whole lot of dollars for 26 straight years (and counting).

Who paid for all that? There would have been money from the US taxpayers, money from foundations, money from investors, and even private donations. Given that what we want — a more efficient process that will lead to us getting better sooner — is so dependent on dollars, it's our job to understand how exactly that works. It's our job to figure out how to make it work better.

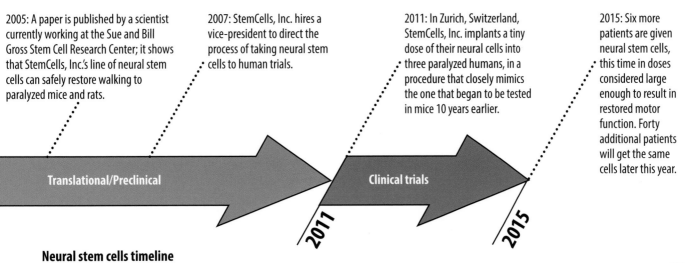

2005: A paper is published by a scientist currently working at the Sue and Bill Gross Stem Cell Research Center; it shows that StemCells, Inc.'s line of neural stem cells can safely restore walking to paralyzed mice and rats.

2007: StemCells, Inc. hires a vice-president to direct the process of taking neural stem cells to human trials.

2011: In Zurich, Switzerland, StemCells, Inc. implants a tiny dose of their neural cells into three paralyzed humans, in a procedure that closely mimics the one that began to be tested in mice 10 years earlier.

2015: Six more patients are given neural stem cells, this time in doses considered large enough to result in restored motor function. Forty additional patients will get the same cells later this year.

Translational/Preclinical

Clinical trials

2011

2015

Neural stem cells timeline

25 The Elephant in Our Living Room

The name has always bugged me. The National Institutes of Health (NIH). Why is it plural? The answer has to do with how the organization changed over time since the day it was formed. At first Congress was willing to create just one thing: a single small office with the job of organizing the spending of whatever private donations might be made toward finding cures for "diseases affecting human beings." This was in 1918, almost a century ago.

Over time that little office in Washington, DC, moved to Bethesda, Maryland, and became an umbrella organization with 27 different sub-units. Six of the sub-units are called *centers* and the other 21 are called *institutes*. That's why the name is plural. It was public pressure from patient groups — versions of you and me — that made Congress start creating individual institutes aimed at things like mental health and heart disease. Spending on grants awarded through the NIH absolutely exploded, from tiny to massive, during the first 20 years or so after WWII ended.

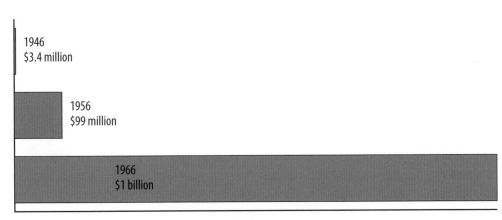

1946
$3.4 million

1956
$99 million

1966
$1 billion

Overall NIH spending

That picture means for every single grant dollar in 1946, there were 294 in 1966. (By comparison, the entire federal budget hadn't even doubled during that same time. Those were amazing years for research spending.) The NIH today has two major jobs: one is to hand out dollars to scientists around the world, and the other is to run its own research in its own labs.

You can go to Bethesda today and see those labs, but you'll need a lot of time. There are hundreds of them, and more than 6,000 people work there; if you could spend a few hours with each worker, five days a week, it would take you about 12 years to meet them all. The NIH is like a small town made of nothing but scientists and doctors. You'd also want to spend some time at the NIH Clinical Center, which is our national research hospital — the place where every day promising therapies get tested by some of the best doctors there are. It's the biggest hospital in the world that's completely dedicated to doing research.

What about spending on the science we care about? Do we have our own institute? Not exactly. Nestled into the giant bureaucracy of the NIH is one little program that happens to be the single biggest source of funding for spinal cord injury research — not just in the USA but on the whole planet.

The Spinal Cord Injury Research Program lives deep inside one of the institutes — the one called the *National Institute of Neurological Disorders and Strokes (NINDS)*. As its name suggests, NINDS is our logical home, but it's also in charge of federal spending on all sorts of things that are not spinal cord injury. To be exact, there are more than 600 specific neurological diseases and conditions on its to-do list. This is the NINDS mission statement — the one-sentence version of how they see their own job: *"To seek fundamental knowledge about the brain and nervous system and to use that knowledge to reduce the burden of neurological disease."*

Just before Christmas in 2014, Congress authorized (and the President signed) what's fondly known as an *omnibus appropriations bill*. The word *omnibus* just means that Congress decided to vote on all the spending at once instead of taking it piece by piece, which takes longer and gives opponents more time to argue about things they don't like. Omnibus bills are enormous documents. Inside the thousand-plus pages of the 2014 law was language that said NINDS would be allowed to spend 1.6 billion-with-a-B dollars during the 2015 fiscal year. That number is about $17 million more than it had to work with in 2014.

How much of that $1.6 billion will be specifically aimed at spinal cord injury? That depends on what sort of grants our friends in the labs come up with and how those grants compare with what other scientists with other goals are asking for. Here's the record for the last few years, along with estimates for 2015 and 2016. Notice that if the graphs were drawn to scale, the one on the left would have to be a *lot* taller; we're comparing billions to millions.

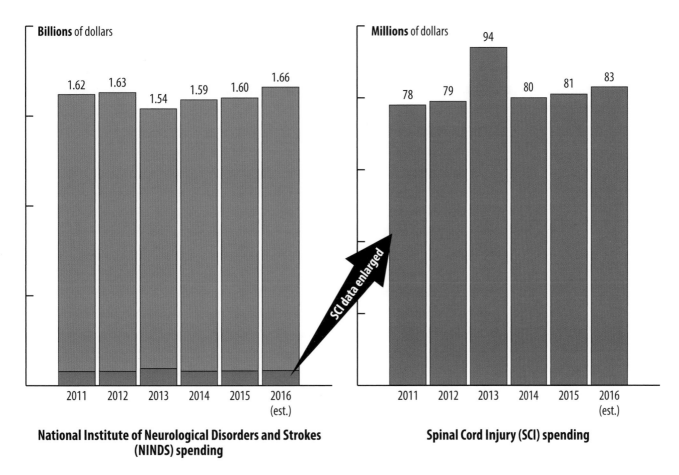

National Institute of Neurological Disorders and Strokes (NINDS) spending

Spinal Cord Injury (SCI) spending

As you can see, the amount of money that gets allocated to spinal cord injury took a jump and then dropped back off during the 2012–2014 years. For comparison's sake, our SCI budgets are close to the dollars we-the-people spend through the NIH on traumatic brain injury. They're close to *half* of what gets spent on studying osteoporosis. They're about a *third* of the spending on schizophrenia and about a *fifth* of the spending on alcoholism. For the record, I just don't know how to feel about that. I don't.

Don't forget, either, that when this money goes to labs in universities — as about 90% of it does — a big chunk comes off the top in the form of "indirect" costs. The actual SCI scientists working at university labs are not going to spend $81 million dollars this year. Let's say that 10% of it will be spent at the NIH's own labs, which is a low estimate. That leaves $73 million. The universities will take about half that for "indirect" costs, which means the scientists will end up with about $36 million. My back-of-the-envelope calculation says this is just about right, given that there are about 250 scientists who will be receiving that cash. If they all got NIH grants, and all the grants were equal, it works out to $144,000 per year per scientist, which is in the ballpark for what researchers tell me they burn through between their own salary, their equipment, their expenses, and their staff.

I'm being fuzzy with these indirect cost numbers on purpose, because they're different from school to school. Each university negotiates to keep as much of the grants awarded to its scientists as it can.

Besides our friends in the Spinal Cord Injury Research Program at NINDS, there are others looking out for us inside the NIH. There's another whole sector called the National Institute of Biomedical Imaging and Bioengineering (NIBIB). This is where some of the money came from that paid for those epidural stimulation studies. And there's a whole new group called the National Center for Advancing Translational Sciences (NCATS), where the focus is on helping to get things that work but aren't (yet) profitable to patients.

The competition among scientists to get NIH grants is fierce. This is what happens. The person running the lab is known as the Principal Investigator (PI). S/he will have spent months working to come up with a way to test a new idea, or to refine an old one. It has to be something no one else is doing, or something that no one else can do as well as our PI can.

Writing the grant means producing a carefully argued document that shows all the reasons why this project should get money instead of some other project. Typically, it will run about 40 or 50 pages. When I read these things I imagine sometimes that this is a submission to become a contestant in a very exclusive cooking contest.

- Who are you and what is your background?
- What is the thing you're going to make?
- Why would anybody want that?
- Can you already get it somewhere else?

- How exactly are you going to make it?
    - List all the ingredients and equipment you need.
    - Identify each one of your suppliers.
    - Describe each step in detail, with pictures.
- Give ten examples of other things you've made that are evidence that you could actually make this dish and have it come out well.
- Describe other dishes that are similar and name the differences between them and what you're proposing.
- Name three ways this recipe could go wrong and explain your plans to prevent that.
- Give a complete list of recipes you've already tried or that others have tried related to this new dish.

A grant application is sort of like that, only it will be about molecules and cells instead of sweet potatoes and green onions. Once it goes to the NIH, the first thing that happens is that it gets sorted so that it will be evaluated alongside other grants that are aiming to do something similar. After a couple of sorts, it will eventually land in a pile that has been assigned to a few people who already have a working knowledge of the kind of experiment being proposed. They've done work like this, so they can tell by reading the grant if the PI knows what s/he's talking about.

The reviewers' job is to read each grant very carefully and give it a preliminary score. They're trying to measure things like how original it is, how much impact it might have, how well-thought-out it is, how strong the PI's qualifications are, and so on. Each criteria gets a number, and then the numbers are added and averaged. The preliminary scores from these small teams of reviewers are what determines who makes the first cut. Grants in the top half get to move on to a big meeting for further consideration, and grants in the bottom half become the subject of painful emails to hopeful scientists.

The big meeting lasts for a couple of days, during which time all the small reviewer teams gather in one room and go through dozens of grants from the top half of the pile. If our PI's application is in there, the people who first read it and gave it good scores will tell the rest of the group about it and why they marked it the way they did. The rest of the big group isn't going to read the whole thing; their job is to question the reviewers and satisfy themselves that they know enough about the application to give it a second score.

Once that's done every grant in the top half will have a score, and that number is what determines who gets the money. If the number puts the project in the top 14%, it will almost certainly be funded. If not, it almost certainly won't. The average age of someone getting NIH money for the first time is 42; it's very, very difficult to pull off.

As it should be, right? We only want the very best and most promising science funded. But, the 14% cutoff doesn't mean that everything under that isn't any good or isn't worth doing. It's just an arbitrary chop, dictated by the amount of money available. For all we know, that cutoff should really be 25%, if the only criteria were strong science and qualified scientists.

Are there good projects not getting funded? Absolutely, no question. Lots of them. What can we do about it? One obvious thing is to insist that the NIH continue to have a big place in the federal budget. We do that by having a simple conversation with whoever answers the phone of our representative in Washington, DC. Mine goes like this:

> *Hello, I'm a voter and I live in Bellevue, Washington, which is in the 8th District. Who am I speaking to?*
>
> *Thank you. My name is Kate Willette. (spell) I'm calling to remind the Congressman that strong funding of the NIH is very important to me and to many voters here. My husband lives with a chronic neurological condition that is painful, expensive, and very possibly treatable if research can continue to happen.*
>
> *Thank you for your time.*

Then you put their number in your speed dial and do it again, about once a month. At some point you and the person on the other end form a relationship, hopefully by the second call. They may ask you for more information, which is your chance to tell a little of your story. You can email photos, make plans to stop in if you're ever in town, get yourself on the radar of this office. The goal is to extend yourself — literally to have your voice in faraway rooms when you're not there. You can talk about spinal cord injury, and you should — but know that it's not up to your congressperson to get that specific.

Congress is who gets to vote on those appropriations. Nobody else can give taxpayer dollars to the NIH — not the courts, not the president, not the lobbyists. Congress *doesn't* decide how the NIH spends money — they don't dictate this much for spinal cord injury, that much for pancreatic cancer — but they *do* decide on the overall budget, and cuts to the whole always translate to cuts to the parts. Conversely, growth to the whole means growth to the parts. We want the NIH to be well funded.

If enough of us made a phone call once a month, we would have an impact. My friends in the political world say that a polite phone call is by far the most forceful way to get through without having to travel. Emails and online petitions don't carry nearly as much weight. Letters are effective too, but you have to write them and stamp them and mail them. Faxing is over. I'm dead certain that it would have an impact on how Congress thinks about the NIH if each member got a phone call like that, even if it was only once a month.

Okay, that's my spiel about the NIH. It's enormous, it's fantastic, it's frustrating, and it's also our best hope. It takes in and then pays back out a simply mind-boggling pile of cash, year in and year out. The NIH has already funded most of the successful science we've been talking about. Remember that project where four paralyzed young men were given epidural stimulators and afterwards could move their feet and sweat and pee?

Some of that was NIH money. Same with the Phase I safety trials with neural stem cells that wrapped up in Zurich in May of 2014. Same with the gene therapies, and growth factors, and Schwann cells trials. None of this would exist without those grants. The flip side of that is, if there were more grants, a lot more science would be happening. Maybe you noticed a couple of pages back that the 2016 budget for NINDS may be rising, and that if so, the Spinal Cord Injury Research Program budget will have an additional $2 million. When I see that number, I think *that's another 15 or 20 scientists working for us. Good.*

26 Money Hiding in Plain Sight

I really don't know how to talk about this next source of funding. Part of me is frustrated to know that it even exists, and part of me is really glad that it does. What would you say if I told you that in addition to the $30 billion we taxpayers send to the NIH every year, there's a whole *other* very similar medical research program run by the US Army? And what if I said that the Army program — unlike the NIH — is perfectly okay with having members of Congress aim the money at specific diseases and conditions?

It's true. Scientists are sending the same kinds of grants to the Army program that they send to the NIH. The Army program got almost a quarter of a billion dollars to spend on medical research in 2015. ($247.5 million, to be exact.) The NIH budget of $30 billion is 120 times as big, yes, but here's the thing. The spinal cord injury program at NIH is $80 million, and from the Army program we get another $30 million. The Army program is called the Congressionally Directed Medical Research Program (CDMRP).

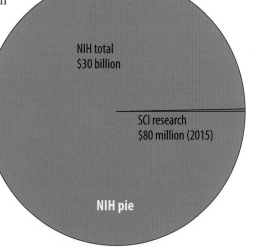

NIH total
$30 billion

SCI research
$80 million (2015)

NIH pie

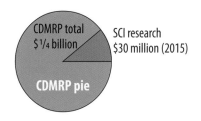

CDMRP total
$ 1/4 billion

SCI research
$30 million (2015)

CDMRP pie

The NIH pie is actually 120 times as big as the CDMRP pie, so it's far too big to put on this page. Spinal cord injury research is a tiny sliver of the big pie, but it's almost an eighth of the little one.

I like politics. The bickering can make me crazy, but I usually like the theater of campaigns and the inside stories of how decisions are made and promises are kept or broken. I believe in our politics as *the art of the possible* — the system under which we give people authority to get at least a few good things done on our behalf. And I think that the CDMRP is an example of that. It's a way that politicians found to get money into the hands of scientists working on particular diseases *without* having to make the entire NIH budget bigger.

At the same time, I can't deny that it's also kind of a sneaky way to do a thing that I happen to want done. This money isn't "pork" — it's never designated to be spent in a particular district (or state) and therefore can't be used to entice voters into supporting the person who wrote it into the budget. But it's still sneaky. There's no argument that can be made with a straight face for having the Army spend Department of Defense (DOD) dollars on autism, or breast cancer, or multiple sclerosis. That's exactly what happens, though.

The Army program funding is quite a bit less stable than the NIH funding. Spinal cord injury money has bounced from $35 million in 2009 down to $9.6 million in 2012 and back up to $30 million in 2015.

If a member of Congress (or someone from their staff) adds a line to the massive DOD spending document saying there should be a $20 million ovarian cancer research program run by the Army in 2015, that line becomes part of the law when it's eventually passed. Members of Congress have been quietly feeding this program since 1992, slowly adding to the list of diseases and conditions it covers. Spinal cord injury got its foothold on that list in 2009.

I think they get away with it because the defense budget itself is so enormous. The CDMRP is a tiny, tiny chunk of the whole thing; it's a quarter of a billion out of 555 billion. If the defense budget was $555, the entire Army medical research program would be 25 cents. And the spinal cord injury part of that would be 3 pennies.

The important questions, I think, go like this:

1. Is the Army spending that money efficiently and effectively?
2. Is the Army program duplicating what the NIH is doing?

Let's take those in order. It happens that I got a front row seat in 2012 for how the Army program works, or at least for how one little part of it works. A major feature of the CDMRP that's *not* part of the NIH is the inclusion of patients and their advocates — us — in the grant review process. Both programs have qualified scientists as reviewers, but only the Army also has "consumer" reviewers. As an advocate, I was invited to help score one pile of grants in terms of how well the projects under consideration would address things that our community cares most about.

This is how it worked. Late in 2011, the advocacy group Unite 2 Fight Paralysis nominated me to be a consumer reviewer for the next round of spinal cord injury grants. After the Army contacted me, I sent them a resume and a little essay explaining my interest in helping out. What came next was a sort of job interview over the phone, during which the woman in charge of finding regular citizens to be on their panels talked to me. The qualifications to be a consumer reviewer are not about the science at all. They're about what sort of relationship you have to spinal cord injury, what sort of military background you have (or don't have, in my case), how easily you're able to travel, and how willing you are to put in a lot of time for very little money.

Once I was accepted, there was a carefully constructed online training program designed to help me get the hang of what exactly my job was going to be and how the process would work. I was put in touch with a civilian mentor — another consumer reviewer who had been through the process before; he would be there for process questions. He would be in the room with me during the actual reviews, too, because he had his own pile of grants to read. There was also a scientific advisor, whose task was to help me with anything I didn't understand in the grants themselves. Everything had been thought through. What they were asking me to do was to read the grants ahead of time and be the community's voice in the room with the scientists discussing the grants.

About a month or so before the scoring meetings, I started getting my assigned grants through email. They were exactly what I described in the NIH peer-review process: 40-odd pages of detailed scientific explanations for the proposed experiment. Each one included a line giving a nod to how funding this project would help the military, veterans, families of veterans, or soldiers on active duty. In the case of spinal cord injury, of course, this isn't really a difficult argument to make. Many thousands of veterans do live with paralysis.

The military arranged for me to travel to Virginia and spend two nights at the hotel where the meetings would take place. I spent one long day in a conference room with eight or nine scientists, a staff person, and my mentor consumer reviewer. We took each grant in turn. There was a pair of scientists assigned to have read it ahead of time, and one of them would describe the project and its merits or flaws. If it was one that had been assigned to me, I would talk about how important this work might (or might not) be to people in the community.

After questions, each grant got a series of scores from a list of criteria, but the only one I was qualified to mark was the one about relevance to us. Sometimes the man who was running this meeting would stop and make us defend our scores, especially if they were all tending toward the same "pretty good" end of the scale. The goal of the meeting was to find ways to differentiate; we were taking the first cut at the pile and everything couldn't go on to the next level.

I can say from that experience that the Army personnel in charge of this program are extremely organized, focused, and prepared. The scientists at the table with me all knew one another — in fact, it's my strong impression that there's a fairly small group of spinal cord injury scientists who routinely pass around these kinds of duties. They do peer review for NIH grants and for the Army program grants. They do peer review to decide what gets published in academic journals and what doesn't.

The Army program is all over the map when it comes to what gets funded in SCI research. They've approved grants to study everything from what medics should do right after injury to improving sexual function to reducing neuropathic pain to getting axons to grow. One of my most consistent comments in the review panels was about whether or not a proposal would help people living with chronic injuries.

So, is the Army program effective and efficient? From where I sat, yes. This wasn't some kind of junket. It was a group of serious people trying to do a difficult job in a responsible way. If what we want is more and better and faster research, there's nothing about the way this money is getting allocated that bothers me.

What about the second question, which is really aimed at the issue of waste? Doesn't the Army program duplicate what the NIH is doing? *No.* The Army program funds grants that the NIH *would* fund if it had more money. There's not a chance that a CDMRP project is going to be the same as an NIH one; we know this because, again, these people talk to one another. It may be that a really great project just misses the cut at NIH and lands in the pile over at the Army. This is good, right? If it's a really great project that's just like another one at NIH, though, the scientists are already going to know it. They're also going to know what exactly made the winning proposal a little better than the one that didn't get the money. And they're even more aware than we are that there is not one nickel to waste.

Okay. Where are we in terms of figuring out how our science gets paid for? Let's start a chart for the sake of comparison.

	Sample annual amount in millions	Grants awarded by	Stability year-to-year	Focus of research	Where money is spent
NIH	$81 (2015)	Peer review	Fairly solid except in times of economic or political crisis	Quality of life, care, cure for chronics and acutes	Worldwide, majority inside the USA
Army CDMRP	$30 (2015)	Peer and consumer review	Wobbly, dependent on congressional choice	Quality of life, care, cure for chronics and acutes	Worldwide, majority inside the USA

The federal government isn't the only place, though, where scientists can look for dollars. This chart needs a few more rows.

27 ACTING LOCALLY

There's not enough money in the federal budget for spinal cord injury research. We know there's not enough, because neither the NIH nor the US Army can come close to awarding cash to even half the promising projects that come through the door. Tight money is what makes qualified researchers leave the field, which definitely doesn't help speed up the process. We need a lot more dollars. Twice or maybe three times as many dollars.

Can we grow the number of dollars coming from Washington, DC? Probably, but we have to realize going in that that will always be a big, long-term project. Having an impact on the federal budget is the sort of thing that takes patience, access, determination, organization, and persistence. *That doesn't mean it's not worth doing*, but it's not going to be everybody's cup of tea. Especially for those of us who are far away from the Capitol and not able to travel, it can feel like an impossible task. If that's what it feels like to you, read on.

Our numbers grow, sadly, every single year. Every year in the USA another 12,000 people get some kind of spinal cord injury. Each of them brings a few family members and friends into this community, so a conservative guess at how many people get an abrupt and serious reason to care about this research each year would be 50,000.

Fifty thousand people, every year. According to a survey conducted by the Christopher & Dana Reeve Foundation, there are already 1.27 million Americans living with paralysis due to spinal cord injury. That is a lot of people, just in the USA, and all of them have a reason to care about research.

A major goal of this book is to reach them and show them what is possible. I'm passionate about getting that done because, as I'm sure you've noticed, pessimism persists. Pessimism persists even when so much has changed and is changing and could be changing even faster.

It's not the doctors' fault that they don't know as much as you about research for a cure. In a perfect world, every last one of them would have the time to follow all the details in what has become a fast-changing scene. Alas, they don't. It's up to us to keep them informed.

Because I've been caring about this myself for the last 14 years, I can say with absolute certainty that any doctors who told you not to be hopeful have turned out to be wrong. If you've read this far, you already know quite a lot more than the great majority of those doctors.

At this very moment a lot of families are reeling under the false, terrible news that this injury is permanent. They're going to struggle through the first horrible months, and the great majority of them are going to believe that something called "the cure" is still a distant, highly unlikely possibility.

I'm writing all this to say, *the hell with that*. There is every reason to be hopeful, and therefore reason to fight for more science and better science. It won't take a miracle, unless what you mean by that word is the awakening of a small army of us — people who know enough to refuse to be quiet and wait our turn.

Can those of you who are new to this world even imagine what it was like 30 years ago? At the end of 1984, guess what? It made sense to be pessimistic.

- The molecules in the injury site that are unfriendly to axon growth hadn't even been identified.
- No one had managed to isolate a human neural stem cell.
- Nobody knew what molecules were growth factors for axons.
- Scientists didn't understand the role of myelin in preventing axon growth.
- The Miami Project — the very first research center devoted to curing spinal cord injury — didn't exist.
- Suspended gait training was still in the future.
- Nobody knew how to map the collection of genes in a human being; figuring out which genes control axon growth was science fiction.
- No one had isolated human embryonic stem cells.
- Scientists didn't know about chABC, the enzyme that breaks down the wall of proteoglycans in the injury site. They weren't even sure that proteoglycans were a problem.
- No one had dreamed up epidural stimulation or anything like it.

That, my friends, was a *dark* time. Scientists barely knew enough to ask the right questions;

only a few dozen of them were even trying. There was very little funding because almost everyone — scientists, doctors, politicians, and people in chairs — agreed that the whole project was futile.

In spite of all that, a few advocates and activists managed to move the dial.

How did that happen? The answer starts with two simple facts: first, the discovery of the drug *sulfa* made it possible to survive a bacterial infection, which was the usual killer of people with spinal cord injuries. Second, that discovery coincided with WWII, which meant that many thousands of newly paralyzed soldiers were making it home and surviving.

And those men (it was almost all men at that time) got together in a group, which they called the Paralyzed Veterans of America (PVA). Unlike the Veteran's Administration (VA), the PVA isn't part of the government, though it has an official-sounding name. It's a non-profit — a charity organization created to achieve the goals of the people who belong to it and support it.

A few years later, some of the members of the PVA formed a new organization, which they called the National Paraplegia Foundation (NPF). The guys in the NPF wanted to get to a cure. I wasn't there, but I'm guessing that they must have been infected with the sense of post-war optimism we hear so much about. The USA had helped defeat the once-unstoppable Nazi armies. It had created the ultimate weapon. It was helping to rebuild Europe. Surely it could do something about paralysis.

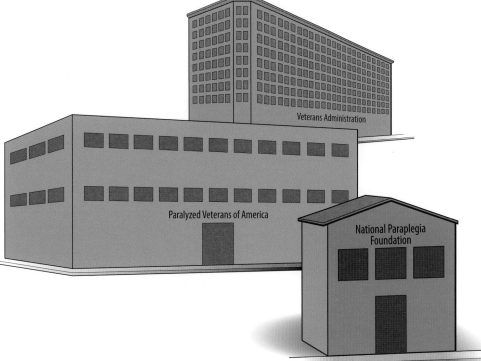

191

It was 1948.

And for a few years there was some energy around the idea of a cure, but it drained away as more than a decade passed and nothing much changed. Very, very few scientists were involved in any spinal cord injury research. Like the four-minute mile, it couldn't be done. Ever. It was beyond the capability of the human body. *Everybody knew that.* The PVA itself had no research program at all… why spend money on an impossible project when there was so much need for investment that could actually do some good? Veterans needed basic equipment. They needed home modifications. They needed supplies.

There was one scientist who never doubted that paralysis could be reversed. His name was William Windle, and he gave a powerfully hopeful speech at a VA conference in New York in 1969. In the audience was a paraplegic named Alan Reich, then president of the National Paraplegia Foundation.

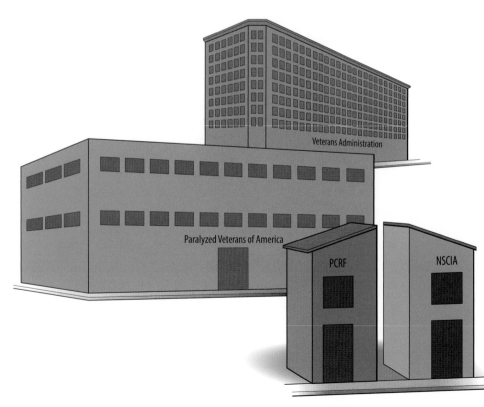

Veterans Administration

Paralyzed Veterans of America

PCRF

NSCIA

Together, the scientist and the man in the wheelchair organized a gathering to be held in Palm Beach, Florida, the following year. They called it *The Enigma of Central Nervous Regeneration.* That was 1970 — the hinge upon which the door to a cure finally creaked open.

Alan Reich's job was to find the money to put the Palm Beach conference on, which sounds like a doable task until you remember that almost everybody he was approaching would have thought he was a bit of a lunatic. He managed to patch together the funds, relying on everything from local veterans' groups to benefit wheelchair basketball games. William Windle's job was to find some scientists who were persuadable; there were only a few. All of them, however, left that meeting as believers. They were committed to the idea of a cure.

What followed over the next couple of years was probably inevitable. The National Paraplegia Foundation went through a split. One faction became the National Spinal Cord Injury Association; the people in this group believed that it was irresponsible and crazy to spend *all* the scarce resources on maybe-someday cure fantasies while good men were suffering so much for lack of basic care and equipment. The other faction — led by Alan Reich — was convinced that a cure would only be possible if and only if there was plenty of money for science. The group they formed was known as the Paralysis Cure Research Foundation.

Both groups believed that a cure could happen, but they couldn't agree on how to prioritize spending.

Gradually — very gradually — more scientists came into the field. The PVA started funding some basic science in 1975. There were more conferences, including one every other year near Monterey, California, that became the main place for people doing spinal cord injury work to gather and compare notes. Over time, research for a cure only happened at all because of a feedback loop. The loop starts when a capable and persuasive scientist does work that gets the attention of motivated advocates, whose efforts then lead to more funding, which leads to more capable and persuasive scientists who then attract more motivated advocates, and so on.

> The Monterey conference is still going strong, still meeting at the lovely Asilomar Conference Grounds, and still serving as a bi-annual gathering of the tribes. It's called the **International Symposium on Neural Regeneration**. 375 scientists attended the most recent conference in 2013.

The point is that nothing that has happened so far was inevitable. All the knowledge and expertise that has combined to make the current clinical trials a reality? We're there because of that feedback loop. We're where we are because those veterans and their allies worked for it even when they saw nothing by way of progress.

In 1974, a football player named Kent Waldrep was injured. He saw the need for a lot more dollars to pay for research, so in 1982 he formed a purely fundraising group called the American Paralysis Association (APA). Eventually Alan Reich's Paralysis Cure Research Foundation was folded into the APA. Kent Waldrep decided a couple of years later to go and

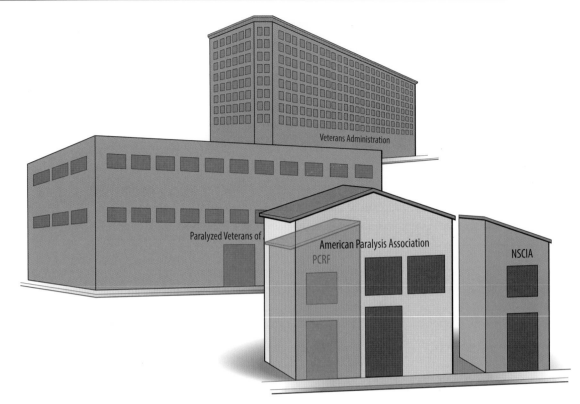

build a new foundation in southwest Texas, where he hoped to found a research program dedicated to spinal cord injury at Texas Christian University.

The man who stepped in to take Waldrep's place leading the APA was Hank Stifel, whose child became a quadriplegic after a car crash in 1984. Under his management and with the help of money he raised separately, the APA began to seed dollars into projects that seemed promising. The idea was to boost innovative ideas enough so that they could qualify for federal grants. And still, it was common knowledge among most scientists and the public alike that the whole idea of a cure was crazy. Never going to happen.

In 1985 another group of injured people, family members and scientists came together to form the Miami Project to Cure Paralysis. Leading them was the Buonoconti family; it was another situation where the father of a paralyzed son decided not to wait for someone else to help. Nick Buonoconti, like Kent Waldrep, had been a football player; maybe the fierce play on the field had somehow prepared them both psychologically for the endurance and attitude that spinal cord injury science demands of advocates.

Forming the Miami Project was a bold move. The center was meant to imitate the famous Manhattan Project, which had been formed to drive the effort to build a nuclear weapon before the Axis powers did. All the brains would be under one roof, funding would be adequate, and facilities would be designed to maximize efficiency. The same feedback loop operated at the Miami Project as everywhere else in the research world: each small discovery fed the engine of hope, and if people were paying attention, every bit of hope fed energy in the form of money back into the labs. Sooner or later, treatments would move to the hospitals. That was the plan.

By the early '90s, there were a few solid success stories to tell. We knew a lot more about Schwann cells. We had the names and structures of growth factors and inhibitory molecules. We had an antidote to one of the worst of the inhibitory molecules, and a couple of labs had shown that the antidote allowed some axons to grow in animal models. We knew the name of the molecule in myelin that made aging axons wither and give up after injury.

Progress.

When the actor Christopher Reeve was injured in May of 1995, he quickly became another advocate looking for a way to help move the cure along. The logical place to find like-minded people was at the APA, where Hank Stifel and his team had been getting money into the hands of qualified scientists for a decade. After Christopher & Dana Reeve joined the board at APA, a strategic decision was made to rename the organization to capitalize on the public's respect for Reeve. The idea was that his very name would translate to stronger fundraising, which is exactly what has happened. You use what you have.

So that's how we got from nothing, to slow basic research, to an assumption that a cure was within reach, to this year, when a whole slate of therapies are being tested in men and women with spinal cord injuries. We got to where we are because of tough, determined people. Alan Reich, all the veterans at the original 1948 National Paraplegic Foundation, Kent Waldrep, just 19 years old when he was injured, the Buonoconti family and their supporters, Hank Stifel and his family, Chris and Dana Reeve, and many, many others whom I haven't named.

They had nowhere near the reasons to be hopeful that we do. They also didn't have the tools: no instant communication to huge networks of friends and supporters. No ability to share images and video with curious potential backers. No access to live online reports from science symposiums or YouTube videos from labs. No email addresses for every scientist they might ever want to talk to.

It all makes me wonder if we, ourselves, couldn't step up a little bit. Here's an idea I've been noodling over lately. It has to do with the way the anniversary of my husband's injury keeps rolling around, year after year. On the very first one, our family was just so relieved that he had made it and that we were still able to be happy that we went around and thanked everyone who had been part of our story.

The ER people, the ICU people, our friends who took care of us, the ski patroller who took care of our daughter, the rehab floor people… we splurged and hired a limousine. We had a driver take us all around the city together for that whole afternoon, and we said thank you over and over to everyone who had helped save our family. That was the first year.

My thought was that in all the years since that first anniversary, we should have been making a donation to someone doing cure research on that date to mark another passing year — both as a way to say thanks for the work so far and to encourage more of the same.

And then it came to me what it would mean if all the families could do that. Okay, that won't happen because it can't. Not everyone can afford even 50 bucks once a year… but if what we're really after is a stable, steady source of dollars to keep more scientists doing more science, establishing the expectation that Anniversary Day is Donation Day would be a step in the right direction. Easy to remember, because nobody forgets that date. Good for the heart. Good for science. Fun to share with family and friends, maybe even to challenge one another. Imagine seeing those status updates on your Facebook page: my next one will be something like this.

Today is #curemovement day for us. Fifteen years of paralysis? $1,500 bucks to science. Take that.

More to come on that idea.

28 Working from Home

Okay, federal funds aren't nearly enough. And as of this moment we haven't built a tradition of chipping in ourselves. Is there another alternative? Sure.

Many advocates have helped build strong spinal cord injury research programs through their state budgets. The most frequently used idea is simple: car crashes are by far the most common cause of spinal cord injuries, therefore it makes sense for drivers of cars to share the cost of research to cure those injuries. Here's a quick recap of the places and some of the ways this is being done right now. All the colored states on the map have a program that funds research for us.

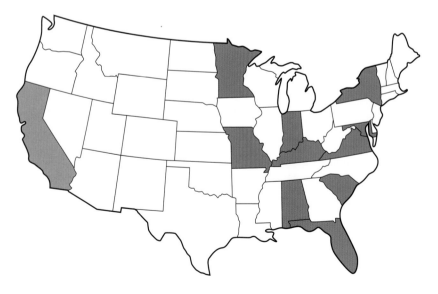

The first program was implemented in Florida in 1988; it's an example of the forward thinking of the people who started the Miami Project just three years earlier. The Florida law includes this language: *"Proceeds of the infractions… shall be distributed quarterly to the Miami Project to Cure Paralysis and used for brain and spinal cord research."* They obviously had thought through what it was going to take to build the financial infrastructure they'd need for the long haul.

The most recent program is the one in Alabama, passed in 2012. California is colored gray because (after 10 successful years) its program was eliminated. That story is about how a 1999 law that brought $1.5 million per year right out of the California general budget and into spinal cord injury labs got the ax during a fiscal crisis in 2010. Advocates managed to pass a new version in 2012 that didn't tap the general budget but rather added $1 to all moving violations. That law was vetoed by the governor, who had this to say about his decision.

> *"Loading more and more costs on traffic tickets has been too easy a source of new revenue. Fines should be based on what is reasonable punishment, not on paying for more general fund activities."*
>
> Governor Jerry Brown, September 17, 2012

It's a legitimate argument, I suppose. But the fact is that generally when laws have been passed to impose small fees on traffic tickets and court costs, they've stayed in place and been very effective.

States with programs like these generally have an oversight board to divvy up the money. In Kentucky that board consists of seven people, all appointed by the governor. There are two people from each of the Kentucky universities that get funding, one person with an injury (or the family member of someone with an injury), one physician from the KY Medical Association, and one at-large person to represent the wider community of Kentucky citizens.

Most of these types of state funds are split by law between research for spinal cord injury and research for traumatic brain injury, and all of the money must be spent in the states where they're collected. The requirement for in-state spending makes sense; legislators don't want to impose fees on citizens only to see the cash leave the state. The best outcome from this kind of law is that a strong research program can be built up over time. Scientists who have a stable source of funding can spend less time writing grants. They can produce more work, publish more papers, position themselves to get more funding from other sources, and grow their labs. More science. Better science. Faster science.

A good example is what happened in Louisville, Kentucky. The kickstart for what has become a powerhouse program for spinal cord injury was a 1994 traffic ticket law. Today the Susan Harkema lab is the beating heart of the movement to get epidural stimulation and rehab tested, verified, and turned into a standard of care for all of us. The very first treatment that has ever worked reliably — in every patient tested so far — happened in that lab. And they're positioned to do so much more.

They have a state-of-the-art rehab facility right on site. They have the human resources to run their case studies. They're next door to a teaching hospital, which means that when their subjects are ready to get the implants, well-trained surgeons who are already part of the project are standing by and ready to go.

And that center would not exist at all if there hadn't been a traffic ticket law.

The actual dollars contributed by citizens are in small amounts. New Jersey adds a single dollar to each moving violation. Florida imposes a $3 fee to each ticket for running a red light. Indiana adds 30 cents to each car registration. Alabama increased its DUI fines by $10, its reckless driving fines by $5, and added a dollar to all other kinds of moving violations. It adds up quickly.

What's interesting is that *every one of these laws is the result of grassroots activism*. There's never been a case where a state legislature just up and decided to fund research for paralysis for the heck of it. The Kentucky law is the single exception; the state senator who championed it did so after his niece was paralyzed in a car crash. Aside from that situation, though, these laws have always (and only) happened because ordinary people saw the possibility and made it reality.

How hard is it to get one of these laws passed? That depends. Our friends in Minnesota are in the fifth (and as it has turned out final!) year of leading an effort in their legislature. The law that was passed in Alabama in 2012 zipped through the process in less than a year. You can't know until you try.

Recently I asked one of the Minnesota advocates — a high quad named Rob Wudlick — to tell me about their project, with which he's been involved for the last few years. This is his description of what they put together:

> *A partnership we developed over several years into our effort with one of the major hospitals in Minneapolis was a breakthrough gamechanger for the bill. Large institutional organizations employ professional lobbyists who have the experience and expertise of the political process and have guided our grassroots efforts in the right direction. Without their support, we most likely would not have been as close to passing the bill this year.*

Directly, about 5–7 people have been consistent on coming to the Capitol about every other week, in our breakthrough year. Two researchers from the University of Minnesota have testified, given advice, and written letters with us. They come to some of the meetings, but their role is mostly advisory

Over the years we have developed a local network of about 40-60 people who occasionally come to the Capitol. We also enjoy a global network of around 1,800 advocates who are willing to write letters when needed. The success we have had is mainly attributed by building a very small group of dedicated individuals, supported by our community, credible local/ regional supporting institutions, and a worldwide network of letter writers. It is incredible how much impact out-of-state and international advocates can influence state legislators.

In bullet form, the elements he named are:

- Very small but deeply committed team of grassroots advocates.
- Active support of credible scientists doing spinal cord injury research in your state.
- Ability to create (or tap into) a national or global network of letter-writers.

Until I spoke to Rob, I hadn't understood that the last item really matters. I would have thought that state legislators probably shrug at what someone from outside the state or even outside the USA has to say. *I was wrong about that.* Those letters helped to persuade the Minnesota law-writers that spinal cord injury research mattered enough to fund it. After five years of trying, that group of dedicated activists succeeded in 2015. Next year and each year until the law changes, $1 million will be spent on research for us.

This is about stability. It's really not different from having a stable household budget as opposed to an unpredictable one. If we know with reasonable certainty that our family is going to have a steady income, we can plan for things like minor repairs and major investments. If we're always wondering where the next check is coming from, those repairs and investments never happen. Everything is an emergency.

I should say that when I look back at the last 14 years, one of my big regrets is not pushing harder for a law like that in my state. We made one try. Our bill didn't get out of committee. We moved on to other projects. And here I am, 14 years later, wondering what could have been possible by now. The frustrating thing is that where I am, we have all the pieces in place here that could build a top-quality program.

I live in Washington, a state blessed with not just massive private wealth but also a humming biotech sector. We have a Level One Trauma Center called Harborview — the place where my husband was airlifted after his injury and where I've personally spent hundreds of hours.

We have a strong local community of people in chairs. We have a terrific state-of-the-art nonprofit facility that offers exercise-based therapy to help paralyzed clients. We have the whole picture, soup to nuts, lab to hospital to gait-training. What we *don't* have is enough dollars to take advantage of that infrastructure. We can't build the kind of lab-to-patient-to-rehab-to-lab loop that is going to be how cures really make progress and how people in chairs get incrementally better over time.

So please, don't take my lead on that one. Take Rob Wudlick's. At about a year post-injury he got involved with a few people in Minneapolis who weren't having much luck getting their legislature to listen to them. Unlike me, he and that team didn't give up after the first couple of failures. And they got it done.

The fact is that as long there's insufficient federal money and not enough support directly from the community or the foundations, state programs can provide a big, stable flow of cash directly to the people who can help us.

It's doable.

By the way, the advocates in Minnesota would be happy to share their hard-won expertise. If you want to talk with them about their process, start at their website:
gusu2cure.org

Part Seven

The Finish Line

29 GATEKEEPERS

Up until 1938, the manufacture of drugs in the USA was a free-for-all. There was a small institution called the Food and Drug Administration (FDA), but it had no power. You could invent a drug, bottle it up, label it pretty much however you wanted, and sell it without anybody's permission. The only thing you couldn't legally do was make promises you *knew* were false — but many manufacturers did anyway. For example, there was the handy stuff called Dr. Johnson's Cure for Cancer, which didn't cure anything, much less cancer. There was a diabetes cure called Banbar, which actually *killed* the trusting diabetics who tried it. Banbar was ruled legal — and stayed on the market — even after evidence that it was lethal had been shown in court.

The problem was that as long as you thought your product was safe, there was no law against selling it. There weren't even any laws defining what it meant to make sure a drug was safe. A drug company could simply give a doctor some samples of its latest concoction to try on a few patients. If nothing bad happened, they could say with a straight face that they thought it would do no harm.

And then in the fall of 1937 a company called Massengill offered a raspberry-flavored "elixir" that was supposed to cure strep throat. Within a few weeks more than a hundred people were dead, many of them young children who had been coaxed to swallow the soda pop-colored stuff. It turned out that Massengill had used an anti-freeze-like solvent to get the sulfa in its elixir to dissolve. And anti-freeze is poison.

The outrage, though, wasn't just that the syrup had killed all those kids; it was that there was no law against it. Massengill's owner had the nerve to say, *"I do not feel that there was any responsibility on our part."* And he was right, at least in terms of the law, because the law only required that he *thought* his elixir was safe. His company paid no penalty except a small fine for its decision to use the word "elixir" in the label. That word was understood to mean that the bottle contained some alcohol, and there was none in the strep throat drug. False advertising. The public demanded that the FDA be given some teeth.

And so the next year Congress made its first attempt to protect citizens from potentially dangerous stuff being sold as medicine. The law they passed the following summer was pretty weak sauce. Drug companies could no longer get away with saying they just didn't know their products were harmful; not knowing had become illegal. It was their job to know. They were also required to allow federal inspectors into their factories. And they had to submit paperwork showing all the ingredients, the method of manufacture, and the wording proposed for the labels. The FDA then had a couple of months to respond to the paperwork. The default outcome was that everything passed. If the FDA didn't get back to you with a specific issue to be resolved, you were good to go.

What that meant, practically speaking, is that the drug companies were in charge of their own safety testing. It could be whatever they thought was necessary.

In the late 1950s, at the peak of the post-war baby boom, a German company began to market a drug they thought would relieve morning sickness; it was a sedative called *thalidomide*. Thalidomide was never approved for testing on pregnant women in the USA, but as a way of gathering data on how well it worked, its manufacturer sent thousands of free samples around the world. Neither the doctors nor the women who took it were aware that the morning sickness drug hadn't been tested or approved.

Within a few years more than 10,000 "thalidomide babies" were born; their arms and legs were deformed. Some of them were blind. Only about half of them survived infancy. The images of those suffering infants caused another wave of public demand for better control of how medicine entered the marketplace.

One of the provisions of the law Congress passed in 1962 required companies to conduct "preclinical" trials before they could test new products in people. Preclinical means, usually, animal testing. Once a company or an academic lab has tested its new product in animals, it has to go to the FDA and request permission to test it in people.

Another provision of the 1962 law was that drugs sold to the public had to **work**. That was how the FDA gradually took on the task of defining how exactly a company could show that its product really did what it promised to do.

That request is called an Investigational New Drug (IND) submission. You won't be surprised to learn that these things are extremely lengthy and expensive to create. An IND is, I think, a sort of moral document — in the sense that it's a good faith attempt to cover all the bases before leaping into a thalidomide baby situation. This is what an IND does.

1. It provides the animal data in great detail. Remember when I said that the scientists at the Miami Project had somehow lost track of one of their hundreds of lab rats? That single mistake nearly derailed the entire Schwann cell transplant project.
2. It describes every tiny step and tool and method that will be used in the human tests.
3. It includes the complete chemistry of each substance involved in the new drug.
4. It outlines the plans for how the trial itself will work. How many people will be tested? How will they be chosen? What is the test design? Who will run the test, and what are their qualifications? What are the outcome measures?
5. It names the outside agency that will monitor the study.
6. It includes a signed promise from everyone involved that the patients will understand that they're taking part in an experiment with no guarantees about the outcome, good or bad.
7. It includes another signed promise from everyone involved that if anything bad does happen, it will be reported in full and in public.

All of that is in place to protect us. The FDA is a *regulatory* agency — an organization created to set and enforce rules. It's also enormous; more than 13,000 people work there full time. On the next page, you'll see an organization chart with the groups that matter most to us highlighted.

Food and Drug Administration

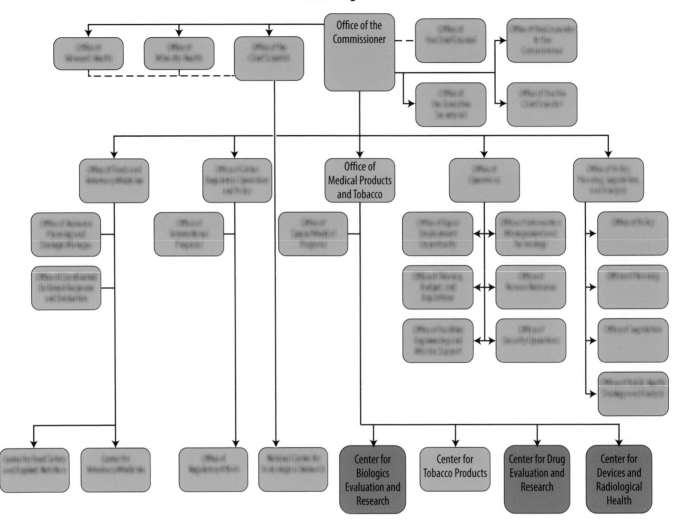

The three red-colored groups match the possible spinal cord injury treatments and interventions we've been talking about throughout this book.

- Cells and gene therapy belong to the Center for Biologics Evaluation and Research (CBER).
- Devices like the epidural stimulator are under the Center for Devices and Radiological Health (CDRH).

- Molecules like growth factors and peptides are controlled by the Center for Drug Evaluation and Research (CDER).

Between them, CBER, CDRH, and CDER employ more than 5,000 people. Why does this matter? Because there's a reason the FDA can seem like an intractable, unapproachable bureaucracy. It's *big*. On the other hand, it's good that all those people are making sure nobody sells us products that are worthless or harmful.

The trick, as I'm sure you've figured out, is to write the rules in such a way that the benefits of new drugs and devices are larger than the risks associated with them. If the rules are too strict, there will never be progress. If they're not strict enough, people will buy useless or harmful products, and the progress toward real cures will be slowed down.

Do we have any voice in figuring out where that risk/benefit line should be drawn? We always have a voice, in the sense that everybody at the FDA works for us, the taxpayers. We have every right to communicate with them and ask about why they do what they do. I have a small cautionary tale, though.

At the very beginning of this book I mentioned the group called ACT UP — a small collection of activists who organized themselves to demand faster and more effective research and testing of drugs to stop AIDS. They were frantically trying to force the FDA to speed up its testing process. The standard drug safety and efficacy testing was far too slow in the case of AIDS, which was 100% fatal, already in the bodies of hundreds of thousands of people, and spreading fast.

ACT UP believed, therefore, that when it came to AIDS the FDA had the balance between risk and benefit all wrong. What risk, went their argument, was worse than an almost certain death within a year or two of diagnosis? They organized to demand that any drugs that had even a small chance of helping them be tested immediately and at the same time be made available to anyone who was willing to take the risk.

The FDA gave in. The problem was that more testing would have shown that the drugs really didn't work, especially on patients who were symptom-free when they started taking the medication. That population got sick and died just as quickly as if they'd

The ACT UP story is told to great effect in a 2012 film called *How to Survive a Plague*. I highly recommended it to anybody interested in the process of drug development and testing.

taken nothing. This is what one advocate said when German scientists finally published definitive, devastating testing results on those drugs a few years later:

> *It's been a huge expenditure, a waste of money for the US taxpayer, and it was naivete on our part to think that the magic bullet was out there and just had to be tested in humans and given to us as the cure.*
>
> Peter Staley, How to Survive a Plague, 2012

The bitter truth was that in their desperation, advocates had wasted precious time and resources. It wasn't until 1996 that members of the AIDS community, working cooperatively with teams at the FDA, finally landed on a protocol to test a combination therapy that worked. I'm bringing all this up because on days when I'm feeling discouraged, it helps me to remember that the FDA isn't the enemy. They have a lot of experience at this by now. They're also not indifferent to us or to any other patient group; in fact they're quite aware that talking directly with us is important. The question is how to do that efficiently.

A couple of years ago they launched what they call the *Patient-Focused Drug Development Initiative*. It's an organized way for FDA officials to meet publicly and face-to-face with patient groups and hear their concerns. The end goal is to make sure that the people who develop and enforce the rules understand what the patients care most about. Looking over one of the reports developed from those meetings gives me hope – they're asking the right questions, documenting the answers, and taking the patients' concerns seriously.

The very first topic in one report is *Disease Symptoms and Daily Impacts That Matter Most to Patients*. Questions in that section included:

- What are the most significant symptoms that you experience resulting from your condition?
- What are the most negative impacts on your daily life that result from your condition and its symptoms?
- How does the condition affect your daily life on the best days and worst days?
- What changes have you had to make in your life because of your condition?

What I like about this is that the FDA is not assuming it knows what we live with or what we care about the most. It's not playing the all-knowing parent or the all-powerful bureaucrat;

instead, the posture is open. *Tell us what it's like to live with paralysis. Explain what matters most to you, and why. We're listening.*

30 TRY ME

Let's talk about tests.

For most of us, that word has to do with school. You go to class, do your homework, and sometime later you take a test to show how much you learned and how well you learned it. I was a high school math teacher for a long time, and I'm going to tell you a secret that most people who haven't been teachers don't know: *writing good test questions is hard*. Lots of teachers hate coming up with the questions as much as students hate answering them.

The trickiest part is to make sure the questions are neither too fuzzy nor too obvious. A fuzzy question is one that a student can read in more than one way. It's ambiguous, and that means you're going to get a variety of answers because students aren't going to know what exactly you were trying to ask. The test won't do its job, which is to give you a measure of how well your students understand the important stuff.

An obvious question, on the other hand, is one that doesn't require any knowledge from the student; everybody gets it right. Again, you have no measure of what the class learned. The whole principle of the teach-study-test routine is that there should be a difference between what students know beforehand and what they know afterward.

Testing new molecules and cells and devices is exactly like that.

There should be a difference between what the patient experiences before the intervention and after it, just as there should be a difference between what a student knows before the lesson and after it. If the test shows no difference, there are two possibilities. One is that intervention has failed, and the other is that the

> I'm going to use the word doctors and scientists and government types use as a catch-all for molecules, cells, and devices that are meant to help patients: *intervention*. A doctor who prescribes something for a patient is *intervening* — coming between the condition and the person who suffers from it.

question was badly designed and didn't catch the difference. If the test shows ambiguous results, that's another kind of failure. The idea — for both teachers and scientists — is to ask the questions in such a way that the answers have clear, reliable meaning in terms of before and after.

All of which is to say this: a clinical trial (also called a research study) begins with a set of carefully written questions. When FDA officials sit down with scientists who want to run a test, everyone has the same agenda — to come up with a set of questions that they believe can be answered in a definitive way. The starting questions are general; they lead to specific ones.

- **Starting Question:** *Does the epidural stimulator work?*
- **Specific Question:** *How can we demonstrate that the epidural stimulator allows a patient to move muscles below the injury level in a controlled way with no sensory input?*
- **Starting Question:** *Do neural stem cells help some patients recover feeling below the injury site?*
- **Specific Question:** *How will recovery of sensory function after implantation of neural stem cells be measured?*

The questions lead to a set of rules about how the testing will be done — those rules are called the *protocol*. They define in general the who-what-when that will guide the structure of the trial.

Who will be allowed to participate? Who will be kept from participating? These are the inclusion/exclusion rules. In clinical trials for people with spinal cord injury, the inclusion rules will always name things like time since injury, general health, level of injury, age, current medications, previous interventions, and so on.

What will happen to the participants? This defines the intervention itself. If it involves a cell transplant, the description includes the nature of the surgery, the source of the cells, the number of cells, the post-operative routine, and the nature and timing of follow-up events. If there's going to be an epidural stimulator implanted, same deal. What it is, where it goes, how much recovery time, what sort of post-implant training to expect, and how long the follow-up will last are all part of the protocol.

It takes a lot of time to sort out all those variables. This is, in my opinion, the part of the process where input from *us* would be most valuable to the system. In some ways, it's kind of shocking that until 2013, there was no formal, routine practice of involving patients in trial design. How could even the most dedicated scientist at the FDA be expected to know what matters most to people living with spinal cord injury? How could a trial be designed without asking us directly?

When the intervention is a drug, trials usually happen in what are called *phases*. Here's how it works.

Phase I is when a tiny dose of the drug is given to a tiny group of people. It's as if those volunteers get a sip of the drink — not enough to quench thirst, but probably enough to make them queasy if it's poison. In Phase I, doctors are looking mostly for things that go wrong. This is where side effects start to be identified.

By the way, people who participate in legitimate trials **always** have the option to bail at any point in the process. As you might imagine, it's terribly frustrating to scientists when their oh-so-carefully-chosen participants jump ship. They lose all the data associated with that person. They might not be able to answer the questions the trial was designed to ask. It's a huge waste of time and money.

In **Phase II**, the idea is to have enough people take a big enough dose to show that the drug does some good. Data about side effects also continues to be gathered and sorted.

Phase III is where the testing gets serious. This time there will be — usually — thousands of volunteers. The gold standard for the third phase is what's known as a *double-blind study*. It works like this: take your thousand volunteers and sort them randomly into two groups. Random sorting means that the chance of any particular person getting put into one group or the other is exactly even.

The two groups are called the *arms* of the study. One arm is the treatment group; those people will all get the drug being tested. The other arm is the control group; they don't get the drug. In a double-blind study, nobody involved is allowed to know which patients were in which group until it's all over. The patients who get the drug aren't sure if they're getting it. The patients who don't get the drug aren't sure. The doctors who examine the patients don't know for sure. Nobody knows.

Why do researchers do that?

The word **placebo** is Latin for "I will please." Doctors give their patients placebos because they want the patients to calm down — to be "pleased," not cured…

Because the human mind can trick itself. All of us — kids, old people, PhDs, high school students, doctors, nurses — every last one of us suffers from a tendency to believe that what we *want* to be true *is* true. If a patient knows that he has taken medicine, he will look for — and find — evidence that it's working. He will feel better. This is known as the *placebo effect*. Scientists aren't immune from this tendency, either. If they look at results from patients they know have been treated, they're likely to see evidence of improvement even if it isn't there.

Blinding prevents everybody from unconsciously tweaking the results toward the outcome they're hoping desperately to see. If the double-blind study is the gold standard of clinical trials, the single-blind study might be called the silver standard. In single-blind studies, only the patients don't know whether or not they're getting the drug. The doctors and scientists and nurses all know. When a drug makes it through all three phases of a clinical trial and shows evidence that it's safe and effective, it can go on the market. The company that paid for those trials is positioned to make money selling it. Insurance companies are required to reimburse patients for it. Patients get to take it, and they get relief from what ails them. Everybody wins, but all of that goodness rests on the strength of those double-blind trials.

I think you can see the problem our community has, right?

This system isn't going to work for us. The interventions that have the most promise for us are not drugs. There isn't going to be a pill we can swallow or a shot we can get that changes the structure of the damaged cells inside our spinal cords or rewires the connections that are lost. We need combinations, and we need follow-up with a carefully designed and managed course of physical therapy. How can you double-blind that? How can you single-blind it?

The testing that's happening right now for a few spinal cord injury interventions is basic Phase I and II stuff. The really hard question is what a convincing Phase III trial would look like. And once you answer that, you have to wonder who would pay for it.

Let's take the Big Idea epidural stimulation project to see one way that this could play out. For starters, the patients can't be blinded; if they get the stimulator they're definitely going to know it. Without blinding, the study gets weaker in terms of how much the people who count — regulators, insurance companies, doctors — are willing to trust it. This will be a one-armed trial, without a formal control group.

Next, there won't be thousands of people in the study, which means that there won't be a giant collection of data. Why not thousands of people? Money and capacity. Each device costs $25,000. There is a cost to each surgery. There is a cost for PTs to do the long-term rehab. There is a cost to gather and sort data. That's the money problem. The capacity problem has to do mostly with who is trained to deliver this brand new kind of rehab and how many facilities exist where this training can be done. You can't suddenly do rehab on thousands of customers without the right equipment and people.

Right now, regular working physical therapists don't get paid by insurance companies for helping spinal cord injury patients use gait training. That's because — so far — the kind of evidence needed to get gait training on the list of approved treatments doesn't exist. Our insurance will pay for me to see a PT if I wrench my shoulder, but it won't pay for my husband to see a PT who knows how to put him in a harness over a moving treadmill. We're in a sort of chicken and egg bind, right? We can't gather the evidence because there's no mechanism to pay the people who would have to help gather it, but we can't arrange to pay those people until there's evidence.

The Big Idea plan is to put the existing Medtronic pain stimulators into the lower backs of just 36 more people and then leverage what happens to them to build the case for a larger study. The Christopher & Dana Reeve Foundation has committed to raising the money privately to pay for the entire 36-person study. The faster that happens, the faster there will be evidence that a larger study makes sense. It's likely that the 36-person study will help build out the questions that a big study can answer. Whether it does or not, all of us need to understand this: those questions — and that study design — have to be defined somehow.

We're in new territory. There's nothing in clinical trial history to guide what happens next, which to my mind is good news and bad news. It's bad news because it's going to take more than the usual amount of work to figure out how to invent our own solid version of Phase III, which is the only way treatments are ever going to get on the market. A successful Phase III trial is the gateway.

And it's good news because we — the patient group — can be part of the solution. I'm not just talking about what happens with The Big Idea. I'm talking about all of it.

The science is, at long last, in a place where our actions can have an impact.

31 What We Can Do

Here's a really dumb question: *Would you prefer that spinal cord injury treatments be available within the next three years, or would you rather wait another ten or twenty years?*

Or how about this one: *Would you prefer that there be a treatment that just kind of works, or would you rather have one that's really effective?*

One more: *Would you rather have regulators, funding organizations, politicians, scientists, and the general public know what's most important to you in the way of treatments, or would you prefer to let them guess?*

I kid.

The thing is, we happen to be occupying a moment when our participation in every aspect of the process matters more than it ever has. The problem we have is figuring out what we can do, where we can do it, and how we can do it most effectively. This final chapter is going to be a quick and dirty recap of everything I've said before, followed by a set of suggestions and ideas that flow from all that information. The recap is easy, because it follows the structure of the book.

PART ONE: THE STUFF THE CORD IS MADE OF

The cord is made of living cells — specifically, it's made of neurons, oligodendrocytes, and astrocytes. Each type of cell has its own set of tasks, and each type gets damaged or destroyed by spinal cord injury. Because our bodies don't come with a natural ability to replace these kinds of cells, they're really gone once they're dead. The neurons in the cord come in three flavors: motor neurons, sensory neurons, and interneurons.

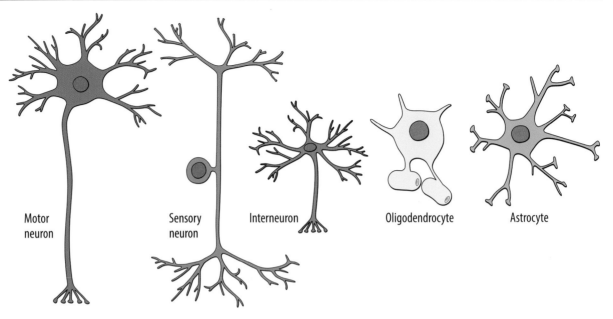

Motor neuron   Sensory neuron   Interneuron   Oligodendrocyte   Astrocyte

Every neuron is embedded in multiple giant networks; they connect with cells from the brain, they connect with each other, and they connect with cells out in the body. Those networks develop both before birth and during the first few months afterwards; they're meant to be permanent. They're unbelievably complex.

Most importantly, with the right stimulation and training after injury, those networks can be rewired. They can be rewired in such a way that the phrase "complete injury" is meaningless.

Part Two: Guests at the Party

One of the strategies for treating spinal cord injury is the idea of replacing lost cells with new ones. Generally speaking, there are two attractive sources for these cells: one source is certain cells from our own bodies that might work as substitutes, and the other is cells gathered and groomed from sources outside of us. If new neurons or oligodendrocytes or astrocytes could be manufactured, goes the thinking, maybe the cord could be made whole again.

We looked at three kinds of cells from our own bodies, usually referred to as "adult stem cells." Those are shown on the right half of the circle. The three kinds of cells that come from outside of our own bodies are on the left half. The deal with cell replacement as a strategy is this: it's a very, very difficult project. Taking a cell that's designed to do one thing and getting

it to do something else perfectly and smoothly is just as tricky as it sounds — and that's not even taking into account the possibility of seeing those cells turn cancerous. It's extraordinary — truly incredible — that three of the cell types on that graph are being tested in early clinical trials in the USA right now.

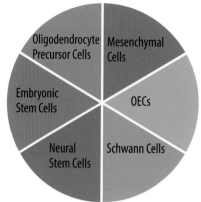

PART THREE: GETTING LUCKY

These chapters are about the breakthrough work being done with epidural stimulation. Every single person who has had one of these things implanted has seen some return of muscle control. They've enjoyed improved sexual function and better control of both bowel and bladder. Their bodies behave more normally in terms of temperature control and blood pressure. And that's just with the "Model T" version of the device; there's every reason to expect that when doctors implant more sophisticated models, the news will be even better. The best news, though, is the way these stimulators have challenged the old dogma about how people with complete injuries can never get better. They can. They *are*.

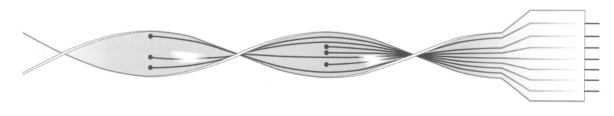

The Swiss version of an epidural stimulator is like a stretchy ribbon, designed to move and twist as if it were part of the dura itself

PART FOUR: A HEALTHY ENVIRONMENT

Eventually, we all want a full recovery. That's going to mean somehow addressing the fact that the injury site itself is a problem. The chapters in this section go into detail about the nature of that problem, which I characterize like this: *It doesn't matter if you have healthy neurons if their axons can't grow through or around the damaged bit of the cord.* The good news is that we know quite a lot about the barrier molecules in there, and we're getting closer to seeing clinical trials that will test ways to coax the axons across the injury site.

There are tactics being worked to address each one of the issues: chABC to break down the CSPG wall, growth factors to add some oomph to weak axons, neutralizer molecules to de-activate the "sharks," peptides to break the bond between growing axons and the receptors that trap them, and gene modifications to give neurons themselves the old *grow your axon* instructions.

None of this is being tested in people right now, but at least one thing (chABC) is getting closer. Think what might be possible if chABC is combined with epidural stimulators.

PART FIVE: IN THEIR SHOES

I included this material because I think we have to understand scientists a whole lot better than we do now. They're all working within a system they didn't create, trying to use the tools and resources they've got to move the needle toward *cure* just a little bit. Doing research to cure spinal cord injury is not — let's be honest — a lucrative career path. Nobody gets into it with the hope of a massive payoff, and many people go into it knowing that the odds are they won't even be able to work in the field.

The things that drive your average PhD in your average lab are important to us because it's in our interest to help straighten out the kinks they face if we possibly can. What they must do is publish their work in peer-reviewed journals; if they can't do that, they won't have jobs. What they must do is find time to write high-quality grant proposals and submit them according to calendars they don't control. They also have to pay their student loans, teach, keep up with what other scientists are publishing, and work as efficiently as humanly possible.

Scientists who make the news with important discoveries know to expect a flood of emails and phone calls from people begging to be included in the next test. What if we turned that around and called instead to ask what we can do to help them?

PART SIX: GO FUND US

Money. One of the very first things any scientist ever said to me about research was this: *The science only goes as fast as the money comes in.*

I wanted our community to have a sense of what it costs to run a lab and where the dollars to do that come from. For example, it should be shocking to all of us that the NIH — the biggest single source of dollars for research in the world — cuts off the awards cold after the top 14%. They do this no matter how worthy the very next project might be. It's an arbitrary stopping place, 14%. It means, basically, that if the pile of grant requests is 7 feet high and the best grants are at the top of that pile, only the ones in the top 12 inches get any money. There could be all kinds of excellence in the next 12 inches of the pile, but that's just too bad.

If a researcher gets turned down at the NIH, they can try the army medical research program. They can apply to one of the few private foundations that fund research. If they live in one of the few states with dedicated funds for spinal cord injury research, they can try that.

If they're at a place in their work where it's time to do testing in humans, the problem is even more difficult. The so-called *Valley of Death* is the place where therapies go to die for lack of funding. Private companies won't invest without proof of a payoff, and there can't be proof of a payoff without the testing. So who pays for the human studies? Especially, who will pay for big human studies when they include a large, long-term component of physical therapy?

Unlike, for example, the American Cancer Society, we don't have a raft of rich and stable endowed foundations backing us up. For us, the Neilsen Foundation is really it. There are other SCI organizations collecting and disbursing dollars, but from a scientist's point of view, the key is financial stability over the 3–5 year period it takes to do meaningful work and get it into print. Very, very few scientists have that.

PART SEVEN: THE FINISH LINE

This part begins with some information about how the FDA works and why it matters. Put simply, nothing is *ever* going to be on the market for us until and unless these guys say okay to it. They're the gatekeepers. I hope I've made it clear that I don't think it makes sense for anybody to do an end run around the FDA; traveling to another country for treatments that haven't been thoroughly tested is a crap shoot. Trying an untested therapy could actually make you worse. It could make you ineligible for a legitimate study or even for a treatment when one arrives on the market. It will not move the science along for anybody else. I understand the impulse to go, believe me. *Resist it.*

I'm going to end this chapter (and the book) with two things. First are some thoughts from a grassroots organizer whom I've known for the last 10 years. Her name is Marilyn Smith, and her son has a cervical injury; she's the Executive Director of the organization known as

Unite2FightParalysis. After that I'll end with my own suggestions for what to do right now, what to do over the next intermediate time frame, and what to do in the long run. Here's part of a conversation I had with Marilyn in the spring of 2015.

Kate: You've worked with advocates for a decade now. What are some things you wish we all knew?

Marilyn: *I don't have a short, one-sentence answer. But what I wish is that today's advocate… believed that they can effect change. But they'd have to understand in terms of time what sort of commitment that takes. In today's world people think of advocacy as a mouse click, and particularly in our case to be an effective advocate requires a long-term commitment. It requires an extraordinary amount of persistence. We've been told NO a lot, and we'll be told NO a lot more. You just have to believe that YES, we can effect change, YES we can achieve the ultimate goal we're after — which is complete recovery from spinal cord injury. But we have to appreciate what sort of commitment that takes.*

[Think] about today's advocacy compared to the civil rights movement and what it took for those people in that movement to actually put their lives on the line. Their commitment was to go and sit at a lunch counter… as opposed to clicking "like" on Facebook.

Kate: Why do you think people give up?

Marilyn: *The injury itself is so shocking — so devastating — that in the immediate aftermath people are highly motivated. They don't want to accept their fate. They have a lot of energy for trying to make a difference, trying to improve, they do research… they're just full of energy and ideas… and once they've recovered from the acute stage, which lasts from one to two years, they invest their energy for a while. Typically up to around the five-year mark. What happens is that after that amount of time, depending on what sort of rehab process they've gone through — I know when my son was injured I read in several places that you lose five to seven years of your life after injury. It takes you that long to regroup and get back to some semblance of where you were when you got injured.*

So when you hit that five-year mark, many people just have this realization: "Okay. I've spent several years at this. I don't see much change. It's not going to happen in my lifetime. I need to move on. I need to make the best of my situation." You just feel like, "Well, I can't make any future plans based around a better outcome than what I've got now."

Kate: What's changed since you got into this world?

Marilyn: *People are participating in ongoing, intensive, activity-based exercise, and they're definitely getting more recovery than was the norm ten years ago.*

Because of that, I think that some people anyway are starting to believe that we don't have to accept the status quo. We've gained this much and we've got to keep going for more. We can get more. So I think that that sense — that we're not stuck — that this isn't a static environment in terms of recovery from spinal cord injury, has helped a lot.

Kate: How can advocates know what to do?

Marilyn: *If you really want to become an effective advocate and commit to effecting change, you have to put the time in. You can't just go to a conference and think you'll find all the answers there. I understand most people are not going to take the time to read scientific papers, but they can read this book.*

There's no shortage of things to do. One place to start would be for people to identify their own personal strengths. What am I good at? Am I a good fundraiser? Can I organize events and raise money? Am I an analytical person? Can I read science and understand it? There's a lot of different things you can do, and it helps to understand what your own strengths and interests are. Your best work comes out of your own personal strength and experience.

Kate: Are we getting better at social media?

Marilyn: *That's a good question. There are experts out there who have studied the statistics and the trends… I think we could do better, but really you'd need a strategic plan and a strategic planner. Somebody who gets how it works and keeps up with the changes, because that's one of the challenges — they keep changing the parameters and the algorithms. Who gets to see your feed, what that's based on, when do most people look at it… it's a science unto itself. I think to get good at it wherever you are, there's a lot of expertise to learn. It's not simple.*

Kate: Anything else you'd like to add?

Marilyn: *We think that education is the absolute foundation of making any decisions about what you're going to raise money for, what you're going to advocate for... you've got to understand not only the science, but — people should start by reading your book. You've got to understand the problem before you can find solutions.*

(Thanks, Marilyn)

Finally, here are my own suggestions for what to do, sorted into time frames. I'm sure you can come up with better ones, and when you do I hope you'll share them with me.

Time Frame: Right Now

We really, really want to see those epidural stimulation studies get done. One obvious way to make that happen is to support *The Big Idea*; remember that? The Christopher & Dana Reeve Foundation is raising money to pay for putting the "Model T" version of the stimulator into 36 more people at Dr. Susan Harkema's lab in Louisville, Kentucky.

- You can send them a few bucks to help with that.
- You can use your email or Facebook or Twitter to say that you did and ask your friends to do the same.

Time Frame: Medium Term

(By which I mean an ongoing, low-energy effort over the next year or so.)

You can find the places where your particular time and talents will be valuable to the movement. There are a number of them, and it will take a little doing to figure out how and where to plug in. This is a short list to get you started:

- Join Unite2FightParalysis.
- Become a supporter of the Christopher & Dana Reeve Foundation
- Join one of the many SCI Facebook advocacy groups so we can organize quickly.

TIME FRAME: LONG TERM

(By which I mean from today until the day we're all recovered.)

You can focus on funding, on education, and on physical therapy.

- Take me up on the idea of using your injury anniversary to make a donation to an organization or scientist you have reason to trust.
- Come up with your own idea to get a steady and reliable stream of cash into the hands of scientists.
- Befriend someone at your congressmember's office and call that person once a month to talk about keeping the NIH strong.
- When you see stories in the news about "breakthroughs" and "miracles," spread the good ones around and offer to answer questions people might have. Contact the reporter and offer to be a resource for any follow-up stories they might do.
- Follow the science. Sam Maddox runs a great research blog at the Reeve Foundation website. Chris Powell runs one at the Unite2Fight website. There's an annual science symposium called Working 2 Walk that's affordable, informative, and fun as hell; I write a live blog from there every year.
- Tell others about the science. Share this book with everyone who cares about you.
- Find the nearest place to you where activity-based therapy is happening, and go check it out. We're going to need these facilities; *you're* going to need these facilities.

Here's what I imagine: In a few years my husband goes to his local clinic and gets an evaluation. His injury is more than fifteen years old; he's in fairly good health; he's got access to a gym with SCI-trained therapists; he's got some kind of insurance. The doctor knows the field well enough to prescribe a combination of the latest epidural stimulator and a six-month course of physical therapy. She writes the order and we make the appointment. Our insurance company is happy to pay.

Just like that.

During the next year or two, many issues associated with his injury disappear. He recovers simple things like sweating, which means he can go out freely in the summertime. Using the bathroom stops being an everyday ordeal. Sex happens. He's able to stop certain meds, and he finds his general health and strength improving. At the gym he works on standing, stepping, and using his newly found muscle groups.

This isn't fantasy; it's what's already happened to every last one of the current group of people who got epidural stimulators. What we need next is obvious — it's like Dr. Reggie Edgerton said, *"For the first time, we know what to do."* And we don't stop with the stimulators. We want the rest — the replacement cells and the axons growing through the injury site and the return of working fingers. We want sensation. We want to forget all about the days when our lives were scheduled around things other people do in spare moments.

The Reeve Foundation has it right, friends:

Every movement has its moment. This is ours.

INDEX

C

D

ACKNOWLEDGEMENTS

This is what happened. Almost fifteen years ago my husband broke his neck, and unlike all the people with broken necks from the dawn of human history until the last half of the 20th century, he survived. Once the initial shock was over, he and I started trying to understand a two-part question: why the doctors were saying he could never get better and whether or not they were right. Our transition — from shock to investigation — took a few years.

The amazingly good news is that he and I (and all of you) happen to live in a time when it isn't a pointless question to be asking. This book exists because of all the people who were asking that question when it did seem pointless, and because of all the people who are asking it today.

I acknowledge first of all the heroic efforts of early scientists and advocates in this field and the people they were — and sometimes still are — trying so hard to help. I acknowledge the hard-working researchers, lab techs, grad students, fundraisers, administrators, and advocates who believe they can change our difficult equation and who are working to do so right now.

I think the evidence shows that the doctors who told me not to be hopeful on the night of my husband's injury were wrong. There is every reason to hope, and more importantly, there is every reason to work for faster progress toward a cure.

Specific people have helped me create this specific project by directly providing encouragement, art, information, background music, constructive criticism, expertise, sympathy, jokes, financial support, or some combination of the above.

Their names are Jennifer Longdon, Peter Wilderotter, Nikita Sheth, Susan Howley, Mary Bunge, Lyn Jakeman, Michael Manganiello, Naomi Kleitman, Jeff Petruska, Marilyn Smith, Donna Sullivan, Christal Powell, Rob Wudlick, Chet Moritz, Jerry Silver, Amanda Marie Pocratsky, Lee Thibeault, Matt Rodreick, Sam Maddox, Lisa May, Robin DeCook, Maggie Goldberg, Bruce Hanson, Reggie Edgerton, Nick Terrafranca, Judy Bentley, Janine Brodine, Rob Summers, John Jelesko, Andrea Behrman, and Susan Harkema.

If this book contains mistakes or mischaracterizations, they of course belong to me and me alone.

Kate Willette